KATHERINE MAY

ENCHANTMENT

Reawakening Wonder in an Exhausted Age

faber

First published in 2023
by Faber & Faber Limited
The Bindery, 51 Hatton Garden
London EC1N 8HN

Typeset by Faber & Faber Ltd
Printed and bound by CPI Group (UK) Ltd, Croydon, CR0 4YY

A CIP record for this book
is available from the British Library

ISBN 978–0–571–37833–3

MIX
Paper | Supporting
responsible forestry
FSC® C171272

Printed and bound in the UK on FSC® certified paper in line with our continuing
commitment to ethical business practices, sustainability and the environment.
For further information see faber.co.uk/environmental-policy

4 6 8 10 9 7 5

For Bertie,
the boy who grows branches in his head

CONTENTS

1: EARTH

2: WATER

3: FIRE

4: AIR

1: EARTH

LATELY

Lately I wake in the night, and a few panicked seconds pass in which I can't locate myself. I could tell you my name, certainly, but not which version of me I'm dealing with.

Once, I was sure I was back in my teenage bed. I could almost hear the creak of its metal frame as I ticked over my timetable in my head: *science, history, art.* Unstable reality that it was, the illusion dissipated, and for a few floundering moments I was no one at all, just someone who remembered being that girl. Then I was me again, the me that exists now, in our blue upholstered bed with sea air surging through the window.

That was unusual. Mostly I am nobody when I wake up, just a consciousness in the darkness trying to piece it all together. It is a strange, free-floating moment, an unanchoring of the self. It is an interlude, like held breath. Eventually it releases, the lungs fill, the world floods in. A reassuring upload of facts. A reboot. I am back.

★

Lately I can't read a whole page of a book. It is frictionless, this sliding of attention. I thought it would resolve once the lockdowns ended, but it did not. It's as if some kind of lubrication has been applied to my choices. I intend to do one thing, but my unconscious shunts me discreetly away. It has other plans for me. I am supposed to be watching. I am supposed to be looking over my shoulder, alert to the next threat.

I do not stop buying books. People do not stop sending them to me. The books become menacing, teetering on every table in the house, massing like the disenfranchised before a riot. Stacked by my desk, they gather alarming cauls of dust.

I resolve to build more bookshelves, but that project, too, eludes me. I am too busy watching, after all. I cannot spare the attention that would absorb.

Lately my hands itch to be occupied. Now that school is back, I take down the hems of Bert's grey trousers and pin them back in place. There is no sense in buying a new pair. They will barely last the month. He is growing so fast. I can no longer haul him onto my lap and enfold him in my arms. We make, between us, a rough approxima-tion of it, but there are always limbs astray, and one of us ends up writhing in discomfort. We both crave it, the heft of his body against mine, but we are overbalanced now. We sit side by side instead, trying to relive the memory of contact.

So I busy myself with hems, remembering how I first learned this, sewing washbags on bored summer holiday afternoons. My grandmother would watch my overeager little hands and tell me that stitches are placed and not pulled. I must not pull too hard, but neither must I let the thread fall slack. I wonder if pins might be the answer to all my straying. Perhaps I can place careful stitches to hold me in place.

☾

The last decade has filled so many of us with a growing sense of unreality. Even before a global pandemic arrived, we were trapped in a grind of constant change without ever getting the chance to integrate it. Those rolling news cycles, the chatter on social media, the way that our families split along partisan lines: it feels as though we've undergone a halving, then a quartering, and now we are some kind of social rubble.

If there were a spirit of this age, it would look a lot like fear. For years now we've been running like rabbits. We glimpse a flash of white tail, read the danger signal, and run, flashing our own white tail behind us. It's a chain reaction, a river of terror surging incoherently onwards, gathering up other wild, alert bodies who in turn signal their own danger. There is no one predator from which to escape; there are many. We are in the business of running now. It is all so urgent. Every year, it seems we must run harder. There is no other solution. We can only run, and panic, and chatter out our fears to others, who will mirror them back to us.

Everything about this time conspires to make us feel so very small. It's as though the scale of things has overtaken us. The teetering numeric weight of the world has been revealed, and it's like looking into the face of God: we are blasted by its terrible complexity, its stark enormity. Nothing could have prepared us for this. We are working now to maintain the basics of survival. It is an endless, thankless labour. It sometimes feels as though we are stoking a giant machine that will eventually consume us anyway. We are tired. We are the deep bone-tired of people who no longer feel at home. We can see no way out of it.

Meanwhile, at the edge of consciousness, we sense a kind of absence. It is not so easy to articulate, but it carries its own dark middle-of-the-night fear, its own harrowing. It's the sense that we have become disconnected from meaning in a way that we don't even know how to perceive. We sense it when we worry that we cannot stem the flow of our materialism. We sense it when the pull of our smartphones feels a lot like an addiction. We sense it when we realise that our lives are lived in the controlled climate of air conditioning, but we still don't want to feel the weather outside.

Those are just its everyday manifestations. We feel it most keenly when we reach for the language of grief but find only platitudes, when we hurl the darkest wastes of our experience out into the aether and find no one willing to catch them. Something has been lost here, vanished beyond living memory: a fluency in the experiences that have patterned humanity since we began. We have surrendered the rites of passage that used to take us from birth to death, and in doing so, have rendered many parts of our experience unspeakable. We witness them anyway, separately, mutely, in studied isolation from our friends and neighbours who are doing the same. Centuries of knowledge are lost in this silence, generations of fellowship. Constantly surrounded by conversation, we are nevertheless chronically lonely.

I increasingly feel that a part of me is missing, the part that is able to sit with the seismic changes that come, to sense them and experience them and integrate them, rather than to merely administrate them. As I grow older, this begins to feel like a desperate lack. There has been a yearning in me that I'm only just beginning to understand, a craving for transcendent experience, for depth, for meaning-making. It's not just that the world needs to change – I need to change, too. I need to soften, to let go of my tight empirical boundaries, to find a greater fluidity in my being. I'm seeking what the poet John Keats called *negative capability*, that intuitive mode of thought that allows us to reside in 'uncertainties, mysteries, doubts, without any irritable reaching after fact and reason'. The subtle magic of the world offers comfort, but I don't know how to receive it.

I have lost some fundamental part of my knowing, some elemental human feeling. Without it, the world feels like tap water left overnight, flat and chemical, devoid of life. I am like lightning seeking earth. Uneasy, I carry the prickle of potential energy in my limbs, ever deferred from the point of contact, the moment of release. Instead, it gathers in me, massing like a storm that never comes. I lack the language to even describe it, this vast unsettled sense that I am slipping over the glassy surface of things, afraid of what lurks beneath. I need a better way to walk through this life. I want to be enchanted again.

Enchantment is small wonder magnified through meaning, fascination caught in the web of fable and memory. It relies on small doses of awe, almost homeopathic: those quiet traces of fascination that are found only when we look for them. It is the sense that we are joined together in one continuous thread of existence with the elements constituting this earth, and that there is a potency trapped in this interconnection, a tingle on the border of our perception. It is the forgotten seam in our geology, the elusive particle that binds our unstable matter: the ability to sense magic in the everyday, to channel it through our minds and bodies, to be sustained by it.

Without it, I feel I am lacking some essential nutrient, some vitamin found only when you go digging in your own soil.

☾

I am nine years old, maybe ten, and I'm sitting in the back of my mother's car. We're driving through the farmland that begins where our village stops, and I'm thinking, *Is this beautiful?*

It certainly seemed so to me. Once you left the ranks of identical houses, built of prefabricated slabs of concrete after the war, the land opened up and everything became green. Granted, the fields were low and often flooded, scattered with cabbages and strutted by crows; granted, there were no real vistas, except across the Thames to the power station in Tilbury: but this was all I had, my very own open skies.

Sometimes I walked down there with the girls my mother took in after school. If you carried on past the library and the parade of shops, you eventually reached a mud track with deep grooves from tractor tyres. I once thought I spotted a badger there, but it turned out, on closer inspection and after a fair amount of excited stalking, to be a black bin bag inflated by the wind. There were footprints, though, which might have been a badger's, but which my mother thought more likely belonged to a large dog. That didn't stop me from trekking down with a bag of plaster of Paris and a bottle of water to take an impression of them. The results were frustratingly inconclusive: big footprints. They could have been dog, badger, or yeti for all I knew.

Was this the kind of landscape that was supposed to make your heart soar? My mother seemed to think so, or at least a little bit. Sometimes on a Sunday, if we had time, we'd drive through it to get to my grandparents' house, down across the marshes and the greening ditches that framed them, and called it 'going the pretty way'. Did ditches count as nature? I'd heard they were full of eels, and I knew there were rats on the marshes because the cat used to bring them in, with tails as thick and pink as your thumb. That didn't seem like the kind of nature that you saw on Sunday night documentaries. My nature – the stuff that existed on my home turf – was the kind of nature that made women scream in sitcoms.

There were also swans on the canal by the old British

Uralite works, our local abandoned asbestos factory. People tended to talk more about the tragic loss of jobs than what was still happening to the people who had worked there – the disease that ravaged the lungs of so many local men. My mother, who hated anything to do with the outdoors, for some reason chose that place as the place where we would walk to see nature. There was frogspawn in the spring, and enormous nests that the swans built, in which we would try to spot eggs without intimidating the birds themselves. Everyone knew they were prone to bad-temperedness. It always seemed compromised, this place where the wild thrived between twists of rusted metal and barbed wire. The nature on TV was big and sweeping and fundamentally elsewhere, nowhere near us. Our existence seemed so tawdry and small in comparison to the rest of the world.

There were places that I was more certain were beautiful. There was the chalk escarpment at Blue Bell Hill on the drive to Maidstone, a White Cliff of Dover, but stranded inland. I thought that must surely be world-beating levels of beautiful, so rugged and high. I wondered, secretly, if it might be famous. There was also the beach at Greatstone with its grass-spiked sand dunes and pink tellin clams studding the shore. We drove down there in convoy a couple of times each year, singing 'The Quartermaster's Store' as we wound through the villages of Kent. Once, sitting on tartan blankets while my mother drank coffee from her blue thermos, I said I wanted to live by the sea when I grew up, and everybody laughed.

'You'd have sand all over the house,' said my mother.

'You'd never stop hoovering,' said my gran.

This confused me, because my gran never stopped hoovering anyway, and we were miles from any sand. But still I absorbed the lesson. Beauty was impractical. It was not for everyday folk like us.

There were other things, too, that I found beautiful, but which I was fairly certain would not have universal appeal. The buckets of browning rose petals I had dotted around the garden in summer, as I tried to make perfume. The red lights on the chimney stacks across the river, which shone across to us at night. The drift of headlights that inched across my quilt as I lay in bed in my grandparents' spare bedroom, where we moved after my parents divorced. I knew that this was not technically beautiful, but I found magic in the way that the outside world could ghost across my room.

Most of all – the best thing I ever saw – was when Grandad shook me awake in the middle of the night one New Year's Eve so that I could lean out of the back bedroom window and watch the fireworks in London, minute against the horizon. Next morning, I wondered if it had been a dream, and didn't like to ask in case it was. These were my holy relics, my liturgy, the collection of memories I kept safe so that I could roll them around my mind. They made my stomach tingle, like something was imminent, something could happen.

Enchantment came so easily to me as a child, but I wrongly thought it was small, parochial, a shameful thing to be put away in the rush towards adulthood. Now I wonder how I can find it again. It turns out that it had nothing to do with beauty after all – not in any grand objective sense. I think instead that when I was young, it came from a deep engagement with the world around me, the particular quality of experience that accompanies close attention, the sense of contact that emerges from noticing. I worked hard to suppress all those things. I thought it was what I had to do in order to grow up. It took years of work, years of careful forgetting. I never realised what I was losing.

But enchantment cannot be destroyed. We just have to remember that we need it. And now when I start to look for it, there it is: pale, intermittent, waiting patiently for my return. The sudden catch of sunlight behind stained glass. The glint of gold in the silt of a stream. The words that whisper through the leaves.

'May I disappear,' wrote Simone Weil in *Gravity and Grace*. 'When I am in any place, I disturb the silence of heaven and earth by my breathing and the beating of my heart.'

That is what I am searching for: the chance to merge into the wild drift of the world, to feel overcome, to enter into its weft so completely that sometimes I can forget myself.

But that is a lofty goal when I can barely shift my mind into motion.

STONE

When I want to describe how I feel right now, the word I reach for the most is *discombobulated*. It captures perfectly my state of mind: confused, disoriented, out of sorts. For me, it carries a hint of gentle dislocation or dismemberment, a sense that its subject is being taken to pieces, their component parts flying off in different directions. Perhaps I am confusing discombobulation with decapitation, but that word always leaves me imagining that my head is floating away from my body. After all, that is exactly how it feels. Nothing is in its rightful place. It's a funny word for a very serious state of being, the friendly face of an existential crisis.

I don't know what's wrong with me, really. It's nothing, but it's also all-encompassing. I feel strangely empty, devoid of thought and energy. I am not sure where my days go, but they go. Every single thing I must do – any hint of a demand – grinds against me. I resent it all. I want to be left, quietly, alone. I don't know what I'd do in that time, should I ever achieve that perfect aloneness. I like to think I would read, but in truth I would probably sleep. I don't have the attention for reading. I don't have the attention for anything, really. My brain feels entirely separate from me. It is empty, but it also cannot take any more in. It seems that it's a useless organ, endlessly refusing to notice what I want it to notice. It will not engage. It just glances off everything, a pale beam.

Time itself is behaving strangely. It seems to have fallen on this house like snow, clustering in certain dark corners, sparse elsewhere. It lays heavy on my rooftop, tangible in a way I can't quite explain. Certain moments in my daily life have clustered together so that they are almost touching. Every night, when I wash my face, I feel as though I have been standing at my sink in one continuous moment across several months. Time has looped and gathered, and I sometimes worry that I could skip through decades like this, standing in my bathroom, until I am suddenly old. At other points in the day, it moves so slowly that I can scarcely believe the world is still turning. Something surely must have stalled.

Maybe I have stalled. Perhaps I am depressed, but it does not feel like other depressions I have encountered. I feel none of the self-loathing that once buckled my knees, none of the urge towards destruction. I am still very much afloat, and in fact strangely content. I am just slow, that's all. I am just empty. I theorise that it's a kind of pandemic hangover, my wits dulled from too little stimulation, my sensitivities heightened by the lack of demand. I liked the social truce that lockdown brought, but I was also restless and bored. Now I seem to be stuck there. Bored, restless, empty-headed and bodily resistant to changing it. Stillness has settled into my muscles, and I don't know how to feel fluid again.

I am far from alone. The people I know are talking about this, too, in their own different ways. They blame the rigours of parenting through a pandemic while still trying to work; they talk about loneliness and isolation, the way it leads them to obsess over things beyond their control; they talk, increasingly, about menopause and the way it fogs their minds. Some are even naming it: burnout. We are, all of us, charred remains. Nothing remains of us but blackened bones.

It is a state of being in which I have some expertise. Autistic people are intimate with burnout, particularly those who, like me, were not diagnosed until late into adulthood. Burnout comes when you spend too long ignoring your own needs. It is an incremental sickening that builds from exhaustion upon exhaustion, overwhelm upon overwhelm. For me, the years trying to conceal my sensory distress and social dislocation in everyday life meant that I bounced in and out of burnout. It came in a different form every time. A sense of exhaustion so intense that I could barely stand; a collapse into muteness; a spiralling into all-consuming anxiety. More lost jobs than I care to count, and the side effects that come with unemployment, the debts, the inability to build a financial safety net, the loss of self-esteem, the lingering shame. Burnout is something that I carefully guard against, now that I understand its source. I thought I might have learned how to prevent it. But no. It has come for me again; I can control only so much.

I sit at my desk to work, but instead I fidget between Twitter and Instagram and the news, Twitter and the news, Instagram and the news, Twitter and Instagram and Twitter, and Twitter and Instagram and the endless, terrible news, and Twitter again, where everyone is outraged at the news, and everyone seems certain, in one direction or another, about what ought to be done. I can pass hours like this, guiltily flickering between all the human avatars that seem so solid compared to me, so sure. They give out steady light, and I do not. I gaze at them emptily and wonder how they know so much, how they came to be so sure. I am supposed to be writing, but I lack the solidity to do it. What is there to say, anyway?

By midday, I realise that something should be done, and it seems that this means doubling down on trying to concentrate. But the only cure I know for this free-floating feeling is pounding my feet on the ground until my sense of gravity returns. There is a Post-it Note above my desk, written in a rare moment of lucidity last week, that says: 'Go for a walk.' I think I ought to obey it. Usually I take the dog and stroll along the coast, but today that flat path is not enough. I want to feel the weight of my being against my legs, to strain against the endless downward drag. I set out from my front door and climb the hill that leads out of town, past the old windmill and between the houses, in search of Whitstable's standing stones.

Groups of upright stones scatter the British Isles and Brittany, often arranged in circles or lines. Known as menhirs, they were chiselled in the Neolithic period, between four and seven thousand years ago, and their exact purpose is lost to the ages. But in Whitstable we have nothing so ancient, no long barrows, no megaliths, no ruins that hint at mysterious past civilisations. Our standing stones are brand new. Erected in November 2020, the eight large boulders stand high above the town on our equally new village green. They assert a green space amid the new houses and apartments that have begun to creep into the surrounding fields as the town centre gentrifies. The boulders are a sign that we are changing, drifting away from the churches that once comforted fishermen and their anxious families, and seeking somewhere neutral to gather our thoughts.

I would be lying if I pretended not to find the idea of a new stone circle ersatz. What do they actually mean,

these hefts of rock that are not even native to this landscape? What are they supposed to signify? I visited them
when they were first laid, and found them rather barren,
planted in the bald winter ground, still crumbling from
their quarrying. I believed at first that they were concrete. They seemed to me to offer an incomplete answer
to a question that we have not quite yet learned how to
ask. How do we worship now? How do we get past the
blunt knowing of our disenchanted age and tap back into
the magic that we used to perceive everywhere? I wanted to touch the stones and for them to return a tingle of
meaning laid down over millennia. Instead, they seemed
to shrug me off. *Make your own meaning,* they said. *We
can't do that for you.*

I used to know a woman who made standing stones.
Jean Lowe waited until her husband had retired and her
children had left home before enrolling in art school to
study ceramics. Vases and cups were not for her: she craft-
ed rock, reverting her clay to its elemental form, re-wilding
the smooth material through the application of fire.

I met her as a young poet, commissioned to write about
her work. She was in her seventies by then, working in her
studio by an old reed bed on a creek of the River Medway,
and still hefting her stones about, pinching their crags
into existence, and smoothing out channels and pools to
collect rainwater. She was happy for birds to bathe in

them, but was adamant that they were not birdbaths. To her, they were more akin to people, figures standing in the landscape like the ones she'd seen at Carnac and Bodmin, eerie and friendly all at once. Jean had a gentle subversion about her. She loved the idea of her strange stones being installed in polite suburban gardens, bringing with them a hint of otherness.

The first time I visited, she showed me a stone that was fresh out of the kiln, its tip split apart to reveal a hollow interior. 'Clay remembers,' she told me. 'It doesn't matter how carefully I join it. The kiln will still find the seams.' I asked what she would do about the divided stone, and she said she would keep it just as it was. There was a sense that the stones made themselves, finding their expression through her hands. I don't think she would have had it any other way. Their crags and fissures made them beautiful.

Like Jean, I always like to put my hand to stone, except that I am more of a collector than a maker. Wherever I go, pebbles seem to find their way into my pockets and bags. When autumn comes, I discover the long-forgotten relics of last year's walks in my coats, each one of them a memento of a place, a time, a thought process. They scatter every surface in my house, too, sometimes requiring a grand clear-out, when I gather them all up and tip them into the garden. Still, they find their way back in.

I could almost believe that they reproduce.

I can think of no greater pleasure than a stone in the hand, the right one of just the right size. Stones have a pure kind of weight to them, like small concentrations of gravity. They seem to always crave contact with the earth, pulling down towards the soil that matches their serene chill. I reach for one now as I write this, and measure it against my palm. There is a definite coupling between the two of us, a communication of density, a heat exchange. For a moment, I am anchored again.

My bored childhood habit involved picking black pebbles out of the garden and smashing them with a hammer. The results were patchy and untidy, but a surprising proportion of them revealed geodes, hollows in the centre of the stone lined in sparkling crystal. I never quite got over the high of finding something so beautiful hidden in something so plain and commonplace; of being the first pair of eyes to witness this minuscule cavern. Later I started to attend a mineral fair held at my local shopping centre on Sunday afternoons, spending my pocket money on specimens of malachite and serpentine, amethyst and obsidian, pyrite and celestine. I think I loved the words as much as the stones themselves, each one of them difficult to spell and salty on the tongue. It gave me a language that no one else around me spoke, a system of knowledge to contemplate and build.

I began to collect fossils, too, ammonites and trilobites, drifts of bronzed clamshells and the skeletons of fish. We were not the kind of family who would travel to distant cliffs to collect them ourselves, so I bought them, neatly contained in plastic boxes and labelled in black Dymo tape. They were orderly, my stones, quiet and compliant, capable of being ranked in boxes and drawers, arranged by geological age or alphabetical order, depending on my mood. Every now and then I'd lift them out and think about their sheer antiquity, and savour the spiral it pitched me into, the unknowable timescales they contained.

Over time, I became ashamed of them, these static friends who spoke of nothing but my own loneliness. I wrapped them in newspaper and packed them away. The only stones I thought about in my teenage years were the ones in Virginia Woolf's pockets as she waded into the River Ouse, a detail that obsessed me as I wondered whether I, too, might shed the weight of this life one day, when the disconnect between myself and the world became too much. Could stones really have delivered that final ballast for Woolf, or was it a different weight that submerged her and carried her downstream? I felt there was a clue in there somewhere, a terrible signpost for my own future.

Nowadays, stones remind me how far I have come – and how much weight I can carry without being dragged under. I keep them in my pockets to retain the simple wonder that the earth can yield, if only I'm prepared to stop and sift through it with my fingers. I've since found my own ammonites on the beaches around Staithes, my own shark's teeth at Reculver. I have an imprint of coral from the chalk cliffs at Botany Bay, and a stripe of something in sandstone that I lifted from the beach at Pevensey, which I mostly think is a thick blade of grass, but which sometimes, in my more romantic moments, looks like the wing of a dragonfly.

I keep my collection in a drawer in my study now. Every now and then I get them out and show them to someone who is unfortunate enough to have taken an interest. But mostly I keep a specimen or two on my desk, just so I can rest them in my hand. In that instant, a fragment of childhood enchantment returns. Contact is made.

☾

Arriving high above town at the new village green, I'm surprised to find that it has become a meadow. It was just bleak, short grass in the winter, but now it's high with thistles and dandelions and a multitude of swishing grasses, caught by the hilltop breeze. There are butterflies, the drone of crickets and bees, flitting goldfinches. The air around me is alive. True, it's nothing like a wilderness. I never lose sight of the rooftops of nearby houses, and the whine of the nearby main road is ever present. But the grass is whispering even louder, and in the distance there's a glimpse of the sea – cornflower blue today. Not another living soul is up here.

The last thing I notice amid all this movement are the stones. All eight of them standing upright in a circle, and a flat one in the middle that reminds me of a sacrificial altar. They are waist-high and hewn from grey rock, with streaks of white and rust. Each is a different shape – one is triangular, another is almost square – and the variation gives them the air of little people, waiting quietly for something to happen. Their surface still feels freshly cut. It is chalky under the hand, as if a skin is being shed. I still sense in them the violence of the quarry, the reluctant cleaving from the land. They are yet to be worn smooth by the years, encoded with different information. But the grass is beginning to grow around their feet, and they look almost at home.

Somebody has been worshipping here. There are symbols on the stones, already wearing away: a yin-yang on one, a sun on another. Using the compass on my phone, I check its alignment and see that it points to the midsummer sunrise. Within the circle, there are the remnants of a fire. New meanings – or new versions of old meanings – are being made. They are as yet inscrutable, but I am glad for the stones that somebody is visiting them. I don't want them to be lonely, these small, curious figures. I sit down on the flat centre stone and drink from my bottle of water, and in that moment, I want to take off my shoes. I do it all the time on the beach, so why not here, on this soft grass?

I glance over my shoulder to check I'm still alone, and unbuckle my sandals. The ground feels cool, and barefoot, I walk slowly, careful to land each tread safely. This place feels safe. It's pleasurable to watch the blown grass creating abstract patterns as it sways and billows. There are so many butterflies. I feel my attention settling for the first time in a long while, in this place that is infinite with detail, with layers and layers of life arrayed before my eyes. It occurs to me that I am resting. It is not the same as doing nothing. Resting like this is something active, chosen, alert, something rare and precious.

The rocks are a little gauche, but they are sympathetic. They crowd attentively around me, heads cocked to listen. There's a gentleness to this place, a sense of peace. I brought nothing but doubt and cynicism and faithlessness here, but I found something that I didn't expect. The stones gave out grace in return for my doubt. They had no answers, and certainly no age-old wisdom that could infuse into me like medicine. As I sit, I find they offer an exchange of gifts, a place where I can bring my troubled self and turn its turmoil into an offering that will pattern the stones, wear them smooth, start to charge them with the life they have yet to fully attain. Stone remembers just like clay, but it is we, the humans, who often split at the seams.

I have lost track of how long I've been sitting on that central altar when I notice a movement at the far corner of the field, and I see a woman at the edge of the woods. She is trying not to watch me, but I can see that she is waiting her turn. Perhaps she is as embarrassed as I am to be in need of a little time amid these new stones, their meaning not yet sanctified by the ages. I buckle on my sandals again, and nod to her as I pass, pretending that we are both walkers rather than pilgrims, pretending that we don't both crave.

HIEROPHANY

Just after lunchtime, when I was a child, my grandmother would sit down to eat an orange, and peace would fall over the house.

In a life without ritual, this was the closest we had: she would settle into her green chesterfield armchair, its seat cushion long ago re-covered with fraying brocade, and lay a square of kitchen paper across her lap. Then she would start to massage the orange, working it between her bunched knuckles until the skin was lifted from the fruit, before piercing it with her thumbnail and pulling it methodically away.

It was the nearest I ever saw her get to prayer, sitting reverent in the afternoon light while she eased off the yellow silks of pith and ate, spitting out the occasional pip. Sometimes she would offer me a segment, but not always: this was her time, her pleasure, and anyway I never really understood. Oranges were commonplace to me, an ordinary thing that I had to be cajoled into eating with an accompanying saucer of sugar. Lychees excited me in their blush armour, and strawberries, too, when they were ripe enough. But oranges were mundane, the stuff of the weekly shop. Unlike my grandmother, I never read their ubiquity as abundance. I had never lived through a time when they were scarce.

Yet now, in my memory, those moments seem heightened to me, a sacred space. I see the relative darkness of the room, the spritz of orange oil rising against the light of the window; I smell the citrus tang as it fills the quiet air between us. I like to return there in my mind, to imagine that I am back again in that room. Sometimes I push my thumb into an orange just for the scent of it, and it takes me there: the peace, the spaciousness of an unhurried afternoon, the quality of attention to small things.

The historian of religion Mircea Eliade coined the term *hierophany* to describe the way that the divine reveals itself to us, transforming the objects through which it works. When we make a tree or a stone or a wafer of bread the subject of our worshipful attention, we transform it into a hierophany, an object of the sacred. For the believer, this means that absolute reality has been uncovered, rather than anything fantastical projected upon it. Hierophany is the experience of perceiving all the layers of existence, not just seeing its surface appearance. The person who believes, be it in an ancient animism or a complex modern religion, lives in an enhanced world, having been given a kind of supernatural key to see wonder in the everyday. 'For those who have a religious experience,' said Eliade, 'all nature is capable of revealing itself as a cosmic sacrality. The cosmos in its entirety can become a hierophany.'

Writing in 1957, Eliade argued that the world we live in had lost its hierophanies – that all things were part of the same flat reality. The numinous had given the world 'a fixed point, a centre', and without it we are left with a broken place, a 'shattered universe, an amorphous mass consisting only of an infinite number of more or less neutral places'. Meaning had seeped away, leaving us with nothing more than the demands of industrial society in the place of profundity.

And yet humans – tragic figures in Eliade's imagination, wandering aimlessly through a landscape that they have chosen to obliterate – still cannot help but retain an urge to sanctify certain parts of life. A kind of atavistic urge lives inside us, an impulse to imbue places with magical meaning, to make them into hallowed ground. Perhaps the place where we were born, the house where we grew up, the café where we met our partner. These places become thin imitations of the holy wells or consecrated precincts that would once have unlocked great wellsprings of meaning.

I don't entirely agree with Eliade on this point. I don't believe that we are now so degraded in our acts of making meaning, nor that the religiosity of previous generations – so often obedient and perfunctory – was necessarily more true. But I'll admit that I'm compelled by his vision of our ancestors walking through a landscape that was in itself a hierophany and seeing depths of significance in everything they touched. It seems to me that this was a very different way of knowing, one that was embedded in the body rather than hived off into the mind, and which was fundamentally more complex than our current habits of thought. Imagine moving through a place where each landmark unpacks its own mythology, grand stories unfolding around you as you go about your daily business, transcendence happening in real time. Even in the day-to-day, you could not avoid reflecting on the big moral and ethical questions of life, because they would be present, unavoidable. Over a lifetime, you would approach these ideas in a million different ways. Our most familiar places would become maps of myth and wisdom, blooming around us like fractals, inviting us into an ever more nuanced engagement with meaning.

☽

Two days before England went into lockdown, I kept Bert home. He had developed a dry cough, and although it was clearly nothing significant, I wanted to do the right thing.

But there was more than that. The pandemic was still a fever dream. The whole thing felt like gossip, and I was worried that the unsteadiness of the moment would unsettle him. I wanted to talk to him before he heard about it on the news, to try to frame it in a way that wouldn't make him afraid. I wanted to say that this was bigger than any one of us, and that though it was scary, it was a chance to give service – to be useful in a way that is so often denied to children. He could save lives, just by skipping school. Even that seemed like a lot to put on his shoulders. More than anything, I worried that he'd suffer from a deficit of pleasure in the weeks to come, and I wanted to provide a corrective. I thought maybe he could charge up with wonderful things and store them like a battery.

The day has a particular clarity in my mind, the final gasp of lucidity before months of fog. We drive to the nearest wood where I hope to show him the trees in bud, the toothmarks that squirrels leave on their discarded pinecone cores. I want to skirt close to an abandoned train tunnel, where I will tell him that bats are still hibernating. I want him to know that the world will still be rich enough for him without all the structures that humans made, to learn to be moved and comforted by the ancient woodland that he's so fortunate to have at his doorstep. One day he will come to crave its embrace when life begins to chafe. I want to give him that. I found it the hard way, and I want to hand it down to him like an heirloom, along with the names of the plants that gather at the edge of the path, and the sense of how the land was formed.

But Bert has no interest in the buds and cones, and invisible sleeping bats. Instead, he immerses himself – quite literally – in a series of deep puddles near the car park, splashing about until the brown water surges over the top of his wellington boots. As an unknowable season yawns open before him, he clings to the pleasures he can take in the present moment, oblivious to the constraints that would come only too soon. And I, as I so often have, hover beside him, flustered, urging him to keep his clothes clean enough to get back into the car later.

A version of this scenario repeats itself over and over between us. I will turn up at the nature reserve with crayons and paper to take bark rubbings, and he'll ignore them in favour of darting between the trees pretending he's catching Pokémon. I will try to name the different types of seaweed, and he will whip them around his head and send them spiralling into the sea. Worst of all, I will want to spend a day walking somewhere beautiful, and he will want to spend an afternoon in a noisy trampolining centre, with flashing disco lights and rave music, and the perpetual threat of heads bashed together.

Childhood used to have dirt under its fingernails. Now it has hand sanitiser. So much of what we give to our children is shallow terrain: the shiny plastic surfaces of soft-play centres and toys whose purpose is so specific that they run out of joy after a few minutes. Shallow terrain has nothing under its surface. It is the same primary colour all the way through. It has nothing to explore or investigate, nothing to modify or fix. It permits only fun, and excludes all the untidier human feelings. It is clamorous and loud, emitting beeps and simulated explosions, the noise ricocheting off its shiny finishes. It is sticky with sugary residue from tiny hands. It is the business of childhood only, unable to travel with you into adult life. Sooner or later it must be set aside, an embarrassing artefact of your past.

The forest, I believe, will stay with Bert as he ages. It is a deep terrain, a place of unending variance and subtle meaning. It is in itself a complete sensory environment, whispering with sounds that nourish rather than enervate, with scents that carry information more significant than 'nasty' or 'nice'. It is different each time you meet it, changing with the seasons, the weather, the life cycles of its inhabitants. It is marked by history and mythologies; stories effortlessly spin from its depths. It is safe from the spite of suburban playgrounds, and dangerous in a way that insurance won't indemnify. Dig beneath its soil, and you will uncover layers of life: the frail networks of mycelia, the burrows of animals, the roots of trees.

Bring questions into this space, and you will receive a reply, though not an answer. Deep terrain offers up multiplicity, forked paths, symbolic meaning. It schools you in compromise, in shifting interpretation. It will mute your rationality and make you believe in magic. It removes time from the clock face and reveals the greater truth of its operation, its circularity and its vastness. It will show you rocks of unfathomable age and bursts of life so ephemeral that they are barely there. It will show you the crawl of geological ages, the gradual change of the seasons, and the countless micro-seasons that happen across the year. It will demand your knowledge: the kind of knowledge that's experiential, the kind of knowledge that comes with study. Know it – name it – and it will reward you only with more layers of detail, more frustrating revelations of your own ignorance. A deep terrain is a life's work. It will beguile, nourish and sustain you through decades, only to finally prove that you, too, are ephemeral compared to the rocks and the trees.

I want my son to inhabit deep terrains as his birthright. I want him to learn early to tread lightly through them without trying to own or enclose them, to revel in the bounty of these shared spaces, their place in our collective practice and communal imagination. I want him to feel dissatisfied in shallow terrains, to crave complexity. This is why I take him back to those places again and again. This is why I insist. It is urgent that he learns this. It is essential.

We carry on walking, skirting the early spring mud. We talk awkwardly about leaf skeletons and trees in bud, the banked-up radfall paths that form an ancient network across the county. We hop across the swollen stream that has surged over our path, and I ask if he remembers how, in the summer, there is no stream here at all. He's not sure, which I take to mean it doesn't matter.

After a while, I stop trying to teach and just try to share my perspective instead. 'There are certain trees,' I tell him, 'that I can't walk past without saying hello. Look at this one!' I approach a thick silver birch whose trunk seems almost plaited and run my hands over the bark. 'He's so handsome. I feel like it would be rude to just ignore him.' Bert looks at me askance, but there's humour in his eyes, and at that moment I feel it: the pull of silence in him that is overriding everything else.

I know it so well in myself, but it usually takes me longer to find it. When I walk, I fall through three layers of experience. The first is all about the surface of my skin, the immediate feedback of my senses. It is often twitchy and uncomfortable: my boots are too tight; there's a twig in my sock. My backpack won't sit square on my shoulders. My walking is stop-start in that phase, curtailed by an endless series of adjustments. I am never sure if I really want to go the distance. But if I walk on through that, those sensations eventually fade, and they're replaced by bubbling thought, a burgeoning of ideas and insights, a sense of joyous chatter in the mind. This is the point in a walk when the interior of my mind feels luxuriant, a place so pleasurable to inhabit that I never want my legs to stop. It's a creative space, a place where problems are solved in unfathomable ways, the answers arriving like truths known all along.

If I carry on walking, eventually that fades, too. Perhaps it is low blood sugar, or perhaps the popcorn brain burns itself out eventually, but at some point I reach a very different state of mind, a place beyond words in which I feel quiet and empty. This is my favourite phase of all, an open space in which I am nothing for a while, just an existence with moving parts and a map in my hand, whose feet know the route and do not need my interference. Nothing happens here, or so it seems. But in its aftermath, I find my most profound insights, whole shifts in the meanings and understandings that underpin who I am. In this state, I am an open door.

Do I see this in Bert now? Not quite. Not yet. But I can recognise how the walk leads him deeper into quiet. I quieten, too. He is absorbed completely in the quality of his own attention, his peace like a cloud around him, tangible, contagious. As is so often the case, he got there before I did, more directly and with less angst. He has a route map to this place and never needed my assistance to get there.

After a while, because I can't resist it, I say, 'Is it nice there, in your head?'

A pause. He turns to me slowly, his eyes blinking as he surfaces. 'Sometimes I feel like my mind is growing branches,' he says.

'Yes,' I say, delighted at this point of contact. 'Yes! I know that feeling exactly.'

'And every time you talk to me, you cut one of them off.'

☾

In Orwell's *Roses*, Rebecca Solnit shares the Etruscan word *saeculum*, which describes 'the span of time lived by the oldest person present, sometimes calculated to be about a hundred years'. This can be understood as living memory, the extent of contact we have with each passing era. 'Every event has its saeculum,' says Solnit, 'and then its sunset.'

Between my grandmother's life and my life now, I already know the span of a hundred years, my saeculum. I imagine it as a circle drawn around me, marking out my connections to the past and the things I am offering to the future. I often feel like I need to bridge this space for Bert, laying a path between past times he can hardly imagine and a brave new world in which all things are possible. It seems to be my duty to tell him that we lived without all the electronic accoutrements that crowd around him, that we played without digital assistance, that we frequently got bored and did nothing, and that we always lived with one fear or another, and that we were always kept apart, and that school was always a hardship, probably much, much more. I want him to know that my grandma, who struggled with handwriting as much as he does, used to have her knuckles rapped with a ruler for failing to be legible. And yet still I came to love that writing in birthday cards and on shopping lists, which were the things that mattered. I came to cherish those knuckles as they eased the peel off oranges.

But that would be cutting off his branches. My son must make his own holy ground. He must find his own hierophanies, in his own way, without my interference. Sacred places are no longer given to us, and they are rarely shared between whole communities. They are now containers for our own knowing, our own meanings. They don't translate across minds. It falls on us to keep them.

TAKE OFF YOUR SHOES

When I learned to meditate, I learned to first take off my shoes.

At the time, this was not as simple as it sounds. I was living with my husband, H, in a rented house on the seafront, owned by a man who had made his fortune manufacturing bespoke sports cars. According to the lettings agent, the owner spent spring and autumn in the lush downland of East Sussex, wintered in Australia, and returned to Whitstable only in the summer, when he could soak up the sun in the back garden overlooking the beach. This was a boon for us, because he let out the house cheaply between October and May, and we were only too happy to fill it. The fact that it was freezing during those months was no concern of his. An eighteenth-century building, it still had all its original windows (read: not double-glazed), and all its fireplaces were boarded up. It did have a set of radiators, but they were apparently installed in the 1970s during a copper shortage, so the pipes were a quarter of the usual gauge. The boiler produced hot water well enough, but it could only trickle in and out of those radiators, which at best took the edge off the cold.

It was fine: both of us grew up in cold houses, and after a while we got used to watching TV under a pile of blankets. I have long been in the habit of working in fingerless gloves and a body warmer anyway. Sitting still for too long makes me cold, whatever the state of the heating system. And besides, the views were worth it. Lying in the bath in an attempt to warm up, you could peer out the window and watch the sea, only a few metres away, and in winter no one was there to stare back at you.

But the idea of taking off my shoes while sitting still for half an hour was not terribly appealing. Sometimes I managed it in thick socks, but even then my feet were like blocks of ice by the end of the session. As the months warmed up, I got used to the idea. It was such a small demand, a gesture that marked a shift in my day. It seemed like the least I could do. Shoes are the business of the outside world, part of the artifice we all adopt when we step out and close the front door behind us. They are more than a protection from pebbles and dirt and broken glass. You take off your shoes when you come home. You do it to keep the floors clean, but also to show how you trust this space to treat you kindly. You do it to spread your toes. When you take off your shoes, you show a little of your interior, your holey socks and your rough heels.

You remove your worldly effects in deference to the comfort of the house. You bring this same deference – this same disclosure of imperfection – when you meditate.

Taking off your shoes is an act of contact, too. You make a direct sensory link to the ground beneath your feet. It is *humble* in the etymological sense of the word: 'of the soil'. Take off your shoes, and you are earthed. You feel the flow of information between the thick skin of your soles and the ground, which seems to reply. I, who feel a current in everything I touch, can feel a tingle wherever I put my feet. But I have to stop to notice. The hits of electricity that I receive from people are far more domineering, and can pull my attention away from the quieter charge of the inanimate world. Most of the time, I am numb to it. But when I stop and pay attention, it's there. The smaller the call-and-response, the greater the magic. You must sink into yourself to feel it. The choice – the act of guiding your attention towards such a tiny thing – is the point. You are choosing to notice the quieter voices, the subtleties of experience.

One of my favourite meditations is to drop through layers of sound. You start by asking yourself what you can hear, then absorbing that fully for a while. The background hum of the everyday opens up and separates, and becomes composed of many different actions, many different lives all surging around you as you forgetfully go about your business, thinking you're all alone. But then when you have heard all those sounds, you listen for what's beneath them, and you find those quieter noises at the edge of perception, or the ones that are so routine to your ears that your brain doesn't bother to notice them. And then you go lower still, bracketing those surface sounds and the ones beneath them and asking what else is there. It's like peeling space, stripping off layers until you find, lurking beneath it all, a kind of silence you can be in. This quiet is there all the time, but it takes effort to notice it. Some people even say they can hear the sound of creation behind it. I haven't found that yet, but there's no harm in wondering if it will ever come into my hearing. As Lorin Roche puts it in *The Radiance Sutras*, his beautiful version of the Vijnana Bhairava Tantra, we listeners become 'absorbed in vastness / Like the song of the stars as they shine.'

We take off our shoes, or we turn on our ears. We press our hands together in a gesture of prayer, or we remember the full extent of our lungs. Perhaps we even arrange ourselves cross-legged on the ground, or perhaps we dance or walk or swim instead. When we want to escape the surface, we activate our bodies, and they show us a different intelligence, pointing to a mind that resides not just in the head. Our knowing is diffused throughout all of us, distributed through muscle and bone, pulsing through organs and conveyed in the blood. We put our feet to the ground to listen with all of it.

Not all that we know is verbal. Much of it – sometimes I think the vast majority – is somatic, the concern of the body. I learned this most keenly when Bert was a baby, and I used to reach towards him in the back seat on long car journeys and feel his foot press into my palm in reply. There was communication there far beyond words, and far more soothing to both of us. When I used to sit him on my lap and kiss his soft head, I was aware that information was being exchanged between us, transmitted through my lips and received through my nose. I could not even tell you what it said. Our bodies have answers to questions that we don't know how to ask.

To tap into these things – to keep that sense of connection with the world around us, to know through our bodies – we have only to keep practising that simple contact between our skin and the textures around it. We must resist the tendency of our minds to tell us that we have already assimilated that experience once and for all, a fixed idea that we can box up and stand upon to reach the next important thing. We have to find the humility to be open to experience every single day and to allow ourselves to learn something.

And that is easier said than done.

★

'Go to the limits of your longing,' wrote the poet Rainer Maria Rilke in his *Book of Hours*. These, he says, are the words we dimly hear as we are made and sent out into the world. They are whispered by a God who can so often seem absent, but who in fact is just waiting for us to sense divine proximity.

Rilke's God wants to run through us like water through a pipe. It's an encounter found only at the extremes of experience, in 'beauty and terror', in the practice of passion. 'Flare up like a flame / and make big shadows I can move in', we are told. 'Embody me.' Our work is to dissolve our boundaries to let in this boundless being, to allow ourselves to be overcome. We are not passive worshippers. We are not even conduits. We are trying to be superconductors.

Not everyone believes in a God like Rilke's, but meditation functions in a similar way. If you have a practice to follow, belief becomes neutral. You will find comfort either way. The hard part is surrender. You can skirt around the experience politely, and try not to feel anything, but that isn't the point. You have to let it crack you open. You have to allow it to expose your beating heart. Sometimes that happens involuntarily. The light gets in by accident. But the problem is maintaining that wide-open heart, living with the vulnerability it brings. The problem is walking through life as a soft being whose skin is permeable. The problem is that you will need to take care of yourself if you live that way.

The other problem is that wounds can heal and cracks can fill in. And that life, quite often, is too painful already. Sometimes there is nothing we can do but close up again, draw in, protect ourselves. Mostly we don't even notice as this happens.

◡

It occurs to me that lately I have been forgetting to put my feet on the floor. There I was, still thinking about myself as someone who did, but I was not actually doing it. At first I thought, *Okay, so I'm not doing it every day.* Sometimes you have to make allowances. But soon it became clear that I was not doing it every other day, either, or every week. Months passed. I was not taking off my shoes. I was not meditating.

My meditation practice was already stretched very thin before the pandemic. When I first learned the technique, I was taught to sit for twenty minutes, twice a day without fail. When I did it was apparently up to me, except that it couldn't be directly before or after sleep, and not straight after a meal. I don't know what it says about me that this seemed to leave very few gaps in my day, once you factored in work and a fairly sedate social life. At the time, I was shameless and devoted enough to meditate in the corners of pubs or on benches in shopping centres, and certainly on the train home, and even then it was a little stifling. It never felt quite as flexible as I'd been told, quite such a natural fit into my busy life.

After Bert was born, it was often impossible. Children get up early, and once they are up, not only do they require breakfast and help with getting dressed, and an endless stream of encouragement to wend their way through the morning, but they also prize, above all else, your attention. There is no point in my morning when I can slip away into a room for twenty uninterrupted minutes, and so – *fine* – I have learned to meditate after school drop-off, but that of course eats into the time that I work. After the school day finishes, Bert requires snacks and dinner and has homework tasks to do, and worries to discuss, and mind-numbingly terrible computer games to tell me about in minute detail, and baths to take and screen time to be managed, and bedtimes that never look like anything on the TV, where kids say 'night night' and put their willing little heads on the pillow and go quietly to sleep. And that's before I've cooked and eaten my own dinner, and undertaken the household tasks that must absolutely be tended to every day to keep the chaos at bay. I spent years feeling secretly ashamed that my meditation was forever slipping. I was not devoted enough.

I lacked discipline. I was unable to organise myself into doing something that I knew was good for me.

It was a long time before it occurred to me that the whole system might just have been designed for men – the kind who had their meals cooked for them and their children quietly removed from their company so that they could pursue their lofty spiritual goals. I thought back to my meditation training and remembered our teacher telling us how he'd left his wife and children to go to India and study with the Maharishi. He learned a lot about himself there, he said. He sat alone in a cave for months and wrestled with his soul. It was hard, but ultimately worth it. He could never have made such breakthroughs without giving meditation his full commitment.

Next to me, a woman raised her hand.

'How did your wife manage?' she asked.

'Well, I'm sure it was tough for her,' he said. 'But she knew it was important to me.'

I'm ashamed now that I didn't see it: the patriarchal way that we frame spiritual development, the way that men get enlightenment and women get to look after them while they do so, all the while being mocked for the compromised practices they create in the scraps of time that remain. I appreciate the value of the monastic tradition, and I understand that some insights can come only from true solitude, but I also see very clearly how it prizes masculine knowledge over feminine, diminishing the wisdom of those of us who by necessity are anchored to the everyday.

I was already there before the pandemic; I already knew that I could not bend myself into a shape set for entirely different lives. I had already reformulated and compromised and found ways to integrate small meditations into busy days, to honour the quality of attention that comes only when you take care of another person's needs, and to break every rule in the book so that I could still find my own way into longer meditations whenever I could. But then the new shift arrived, and with it a whole other set of constraints and distractions. Everybody in the house at once, everybody trying to work, everybody stressed and overwhelmed and scared. H was at home, but still expected to work for eight consecutive hours a day, paying full attention. He was also occupying my desk. I had to fit around that.

For my own work, I was left with the early mornings and the battered ends of the day, and – theoretically – Saturdays and Sundays, too. It became obvious early on that Bert needed to feel the reassurance of all three of us together as much as possible, for mealtimes and walks, and for playing board games and watching movies on the TV. He needed some of his life to feel like it wasn't an emergency. I completely understood. An awful lot of things went to hell during that time, and what was left of my dwindling meditation practice was just one of them. I have never fought with H like we fought during those months. Something savage was revealed in us. We were in competition for scarce resources, and the greatest of these was time.

Few of the wise souls who have devoted years to contemplating the structure of the cosmos could tell us how to practise in circumstances like this. I want them to come and learn what I know, too, and what many other patient souls could share. I want them to experience the discipline of forever being pulled away from the interior, always feeling that the work of the mind and the body is just out of reach. They would have to live through the exhaustion and the frustration and the isolation, and choose to wholeheartedly give care over and over again, rather than to walk away. I want them to strive to attain the mental and physical discipline of getting out of bed in the middle of the night and still find gentleness rather than fury. I want them to understand that they know nothing until they have endured endless spiritual deferment, the balm of contemplation forever at one remove.

We have to fight for our ability to pay attention. It is not given. It does not assert itself as a need until it's far too late. I am only just beginning to understand that my burnout was the result of multiple losses, each one of which seemed so small that I thought it didn't matter. I willingly surrendered my meditation time because I thought it would be a vanity to demand it. I gave up reading and time alone and long hot baths and walking. I gave up silence, and standing in the garden at sunrise. I let those moments become overrun by work and care, and I was surprised to find that, without them, there was nothing left of me.

'Don't let yourself lose me,' says Rilke's God. I feel a little short-changed by this. I need to know how to avoid the loss in the first place. I need instructions for re-enchantment.

☾

As a child, I would look out of the window on a nighttime drive and think the moon was following us. From my vantage point, she seemed to be chasing us along the sky, breathlessly trying to keep up. Later I learned it was just because she was so big that it felt like she was everywhere, and that I was small with an outsize sense of my own importance. Still, I was left with the impression that the moon had a certain constancy. It seemed that she was attentive to my needs, concernedly checking in. Sometimes I felt like I needed her gaze.

As I got older, I noticed more about how she waxes and wanes, and I began to remodel her in my mind: perhaps she was just like me, sometimes round with power and sometimes dissolving into the sky, eternally shifting shape, restless. By then, I no longer thought I was the centre of the universe, and so it felt as though the moon needed me to notice her, too. Our relationship was reciprocal. When I stepped outside at night, we witnessed each other, and that was all that needed to happen. I couldn't ask the moon for anything. But between us, it felt like an exchange of information between two entities who know what it is to endure constant change.

Lately I have returned to my silent conversations with the moon. I go outside each night when everyone is sleeping, and I try to transmit the depth of my longing for my own self back again, for time not to work, but to simply exist; for the right to feel curiosity again, without the sense that it would only make everything harder. These feel like small, stupid things to ask for when there is so much suffering in the world, but behind them is the wider mesh in which I'm embedded. My mother is in another country and in frail health. My husband is defending something bigger than just his working hours, some unhappiness that seems to spiral beyond his control. My son recently told me that he can't remember life before pandemics and lockdowns; they now form his baseline understanding of how life operates. And so really, beneath it all, what I tell the moon is this: I wish I knew how to keep my people safe. I wish I knew what to do.

The moon is an excellent confidante, but there is only so much she can do. Danger, when it is always imminent, does harm. It doesn't need to actually arrive. You exhaust yourself in the act of forever looking over your shoulder. Your body readies itself to fight and never quite discharges that chemical cocktail. You channel it instead into anger and self-pity and anxiety and hopelessness. You divert it into work. But really what you do, with every fibre of your being, is watch. You are incessantly, exhaustingly alert. You don't dare ever let up, just in case the danger takes advantage of your inattention. I've forgotten what it feels like to have space in my brain for anything other than watching. For a long time I kept working – teaching, pitching articles, writing editorial reports – and for a while, that felt like a life raft. But then, incrementally, it became impossible. I was aware of a fog descending, a seizing of the gears, but it seemed diffuse until now.

One night I press the button on my electric toothbrush to find it with only the lowest burr of its battery left. The engine inside could barely shift the bristles. I see it clearly for the first time: this is me. I am out of charge. I've been leaking out energy for too long, and I don't know how to get it back again.

Waking in the middle of that night, I remember something that I used to do. I pad downstairs to greet the moon, and then sit in a garden chair and kick off my slippers. I let my bare feet make contact with the cold patio tiles, and I feel the tingle of exchange between the earth and me, the instant reciprocity. I close my eyes and let my mind sink downwards. I relieve myself of the duty to search for language. I let myself feel instead.

I sit there, embodied, immersed in the relief of it.

As the moon keeps watch, I wonder how I could possibly have forgotten this.

And I wonder how I can remember it again.

WATER

UNLEARNING

Late afternoon on a Saturday, and the sea is a quilt of wave crests. I am quite alone. I unfold my towel and it blows out sideways like a flag. I have to weight it down with stones so that it won't be carried off altogether. I like this. It's proof of my boldness, my daring. I crunch across the pebbles in bare feet and laugh when I am nearly knocked over in the shallows.

In rough seas, the trick is to stay close to shore, where the currents are at least predictable. I learned this last summer, when I swam too far out on a snappy day and found myself drifting uncontrollably along the coast. I had to fight to get back in, and when I finally did, I took an embarrassing walk back in a wet swimsuit to my abandoned bag and towel, for what felt like miles. Along the way, a man approached me.

'I saw you out there,' he said. 'Looks like you were struggling.'

'I was fine,' I replied somewhat tartly. 'I swim here all the time.'

But I was not fine. I was rattled and cold, and my legs

ached from kicking myself back to safety. Mostly I was angry with him for noticing. I wanted to scold him for thinking he saw a swimmer in trouble and not calling the lifeboat, but equally, I was distinctly relieved that he hadn't done that.

If I took something from that day, it was not to avoid swimming in high winds; it was to avoid making a fool of myself in front of the kind of men who sit on the beach drinking beer and *commenting*. Back now, on my own again in gusty weather, I launch in and thrill at the violent rise and fall of the water. There are days when you swim and barely seem to get wet at all, and days when swimming drenches you, water piling in over your head and rushing into your mouth and nose.

Today is a drenching day, with spray constantly buffeting my face and the wind in my ears. I am bobbing on the surface like a bottle, thrown in different directions. It's hard to orient myself between waves. I am just blinking the water out of my eyes when the next one hits, spinning me again. When I finally manage to clear my vision, I see, quite unexpectedly, that I am looming close to one of the enormous wooden structures that divide the beach into strips, close enough to feel a premonition of my cheek lashing against it.

I turn and manage to kick awkwardly away, only to be drawn irresistibly towards it again. I know I need to get out of the water now, but first I have to get clear of the groyne, and I can't. The tide is on the retreat, and although each wave tosses me forward, I am also sucked backwards before it arrives. Everything is moving at a diagonal to the beach. This is ridiculous: I'm only a few yards away from solid ground, but it's so hard to get there. I turn and begin to swim against the current, and I think I am making progress. Perhaps this is a passive process. Perhaps, if I can just stay afloat, I will wash in like flotsam. Whole tree trunks arrive on the beach this way and, once, a chintz sofa. Surely I can, too.

But I feel pain in my knees and realise they are grinding against the woodwork. I'm getting nowhere. Less than nowhere; I am being dragged to where the wind is going. My will – my desire to reconnect with the sweet, solid earth – is irrelevant. I push off again and immediately feel my shoulder make contact with a post. My heart is beating in my throat. I am breathless with effort. This thing – this place – is my lifelong friend, but it is stronger than me and so much bigger that I can't get its attention.

If I can't swim to safety, then I will have to climb. I allow myself to bounce into the wave break again, but this time I cling to the wood, two hands gripping the top and my feet braced against the side. From there, I reach down a tentative shin to steady myself and I crawl back across it on bloodied knees until I reach dry land. I sit down on the stones and drape a towel over my head. I cannot tell whether I am shaking from the effort or just from relief.

Strangely, in the aftermath, I don't feel like a survivor. I feel as though I've embarrassed myself.

☾

The lung-shrivelling hit of chlorine carried on warm air, dimpled tiles underfoot, the unsteady clunk of a changing cubicle. Swimsuit, bathing cap, goggles. A pound for the locker. Socks tucked into shoes, coat and bag stacked, key turned, the rubber band around my wrist. A rinse under the spluttering shower.

And then I'm in. The water is too warm, too blue, too full of people. But this is where I have to be if I am going to learn to swim again. Once a week on a Monday, at 6.30 p.m., I place myself in the hands of Wendy, who is dismantling everything I ever knew about swimming. Which, it turns out, wasn't much in the first place. I have always swum, but I've never learned to do it properly. I suppose I just worked it out for myself. It always felt good enough to me. I was a confident swimmer. But lately I've been forced to accept that perhaps this was misplaced.

I used to think that I had the necessary extra kick to get out of trouble if I needed to. Now I'm not so sure. I've become timid at the water's edge, weighing up the risk of rip tides and cold shock, and that prevarication often counsels me against getting in at all. This, you might say, is basic self-preservation, and it's true that perhaps my instincts are becoming better calibrated. That's no bad thing. And yet I've noticed that I often decide against a swim that others in my group enthusiastically take. This may mean that they're all more foolish than I am (and believe me, I have told myself this to bury my shame when I'm left standing on the shore). A more realistic interpretation is either that my calibration is slightly off or my skill set is lacking. I need to know that I can fight my way out of the moments that I can't predict – those sudden undercurrents that sometimes suck towards the harbour; the storm fronts that rage in without notice; the summer jet-skiers whom we all suspect of loading up at the local pub before blazing across the estuary. At those moments, I want to be certain that my stroke can save me.

'The problem,' I tell Wendy when she asks why I've joined her class, 'is that I can't do the front crawl.'

'What do you tend to swim when you get in the pool?' she asks.

'Breaststroke,' I say. 'My breaststroke's pretty good . . .' I pause, realising the enormity of what I've just said to a trained swimming instructor. 'I mean, it's reasonable. I can keep going for a long time.' I'm grasping now, desperate to show that I haven't overestimated my abilities. 'I put my head under and everything.'

Wendy nods. 'Can you backstroke?'

'Oh yes,' I say, 'that's fine.' I tense again. I don't mean fine in the sense that she would mean fine. Fine to Wendy probably means I could hold my own in a swimming gala. Fine to me means I can stay afloat, and I don't care much about it anyway.

'It's just that when I front crawl, I can only manage a length before I'm exhausted, and all the while I'm doing it, I feel like I might die.'

'Okay then,' says Wendy, who isn't giving much away. 'Let's see your breaststroke first.' I get into the pool and push off from the side, trying to remember not to swivel my legs as I kick, wondering where my arms should rightly go after I've fanned them sideways. As I surface at the far end, Wendy calls, 'Okay, backstroke!' and I flip over and begin to windmill my arms, uncertain of where I should place my head. Wherever it ought to be, it isn't here; I have dipped it back too far and now I've taken water into my nose, which in turn makes me veer sideways under the rope that separates the lanes.

I giggle and straighten myself, but now I can't stop laughing. I'm so utterly ridiculous. What on earth am I doing here? The last time I had a swimming lesson, I was four years old. After I refused to put my head under water, the teacher tipped a bucket of water over me, and my mother hooked me out in great indignation. Here I am, back again nearly forty years later, inexplicably boasting that I can do it now – can dip beneath the surface as I let out a breath – and yet my legs don't want to kick like they used to, and my arms won't turn a full circle in their sockets because I've ruined my shoulders through too many years of sitting in front of a laptop, typing.

I reach the shallow end, and Wendy says, 'Well, it looks like you enjoyed that. Shall we try the front crawl?'

I draw a breath. All right then. I launch forwards with my arms forming a peak in front of me, and then try to cut them into the water, one by one. Every third splash, I tip my head sideways to breathe. I pulse my legs and try not to let my feet protrude above the surface of the water. I straighten my body so that I don't dip in the middle. A cramped part of my psyche believes that I will reach the other side and Wendy will applaud and tell me that my front crawl is perfect – *textbook*, she will put it – and that I have no need for these classes. *Go back into the pool and build up strength!* says imaginary Wendy. *And have some faith in yourself while you're at it!*

But I am tired already, and I have made it only three-quarters of the way down the pool. I flip my head up in a unorthodox way to see how far I have left to go. 'Nearly there,' says Wendy, and I wish she would be meaner so that I could hate her. Perhaps if she could just tip a bucket of water over my head I could be justifiably outraged, and we could call this whole thing off.

But I reach the bar at the deep end and greedily heave air into my lungs. I lift my swimming cap to let the water out of my ears and shake my head. 'Good!' says Wendy. 'We'll start with the front crawl, and move on to the other two in due course.'

Twenty minutes later, when my lesson ends, I exit jelly-legged. I feel as though I have barely swum at all. I have paddled up and down the pool clutching a float and kicking my legs, which is harder than it looks. I have attempted to glide along the surface of the water with something called a swim buoy – an anvil-shaped float – clamped between my thighs. I have tried to obey entreaties to lift my elbows higher; no, higher; no, *higher!* and to straighten my wrists as my fingertips meet the surface of the water, and I am fairly certain I have failed, but Wendy has stopped mentioning it for now out of kindness. I have made an attempt to put the whole thing together – the torso, the legs, the elbows, the wrists – and in the process have discovered that I am now substantially less than the sum of my parts. I take ten strokes and realise I have quite forgotten to breathe. I am in inexplicable pain somewhere behind my armpits. I am entirely deconstructed, not just as a swimmer, but as a human being.

'The next lesson will make it even worse,' says Wendy cheerfully as I hobble towards the changing room. 'In about five weeks, you might remember how to swim again.'

I want to throw up my hands and say, *Let's stop this here. I'm clearly not cut out to be a swimmer*. But I know that's just my ego talking. I've been thrown off balance, as I so often am. It takes humility to get through a process like this, and that's what I'm trying to gather about me right now. If I want to swim better, I need to know nothing – be nothing – for a while. I need to put myself into somebody else's hands and allow them to reform me. I need to let go of the part of me that knows better, the part of me that thinks I'm doing it right, the part of me that wants everyone else to believe I'm perfect.

I'm not learning so much as unlearning.

It is a strange business, this unlearning. I am not a beginner. I am further back than that, burdened with the work of forgetting what I thought I already knew. It is not a simple matter of thought, of replacing old facts with new. I am instead wrestling with my own muscle memory, trying to unravel my bodily notion of what it is to swim. Daunted and determined all at once, I return to the pool every week, and each time my stroke becomes more chaotic. I try to break it down into its component parts, and each of them is possible, but together they are not. In fact, every time I get one right, all the others are knocked out of line.

I'm not sure you can do this gradually. Instead, I think you have to keep turning up and waiting for a revelation. That's what seems to happen in my class: one week, a swimmer will be as stuttering as I am, and the next, quite suddenly, they will effect an effortless stroke and cut through the water like clockwork. Every now and then, I glimpse this in myself. For a few luxurious seconds, my mind and body will cooperate, and I will feel the lightness of it, the sense that many rhythms are synchronising into something that feels like a flow. But it soon collapses. My various rhythms are all minutely out of step with each other. They can line up for only a few beats before they peel apart again.

My learning is like the swing of a pendulum, lurching from one extreme to the other, but gradually it begins to stabilise. Fewer and fewer things go wrong. I begin to have insight into what I ought to do. There is one single glorious week when I swim a whole length with my legs and my arms all working together, and Wendy leans over the edge of the pool to say, 'I think you've got it.' I go home, hopeful that I am, after all, a swimmer. I start to wonder if I shouldn't sign up for some grand gesture, a race or a sponsored long-distance swim, just to make sure I keep on pushing towards my goal. And then, with my whole being on the cusp of something new, the first lock-down is announced.

In the tight, worried pandemic months that follow, we are not even allowed to enter the sea. I try to convince myself that my learning is on hold, just for now, but my brain has other ideas. The idea of swimming sloshes around my mind like cross-cutting waves. Stuck on dry land, I still cannot stop rehearsing the new movements my body was just coming to know. I stand in the living room and show my family my new stroke: I bend forward, spike up my elbows and let them rise until my forearms can't resist but to fall towards my head. I reach into the imaginary water. I explain how I need to cut the meniscus at a forty-five-degree angle to minimise friction. I feel my legs twitch to kick.

I spend my days humming Joni Mitchell's 'Blue'. At night, I swim through my dreams. Sometimes in these dreams, I am hopeless, dangerously incapable of finding any stroke at all, and the turn of my arms is like the grinding of gears. I wake having taken on water. Other times, I am gliding through the waves like a yacht, my whole body working in concert to produce a smooth, efficient stroke. I'm impressed by these dreams. Some part of my brain has taken over the act of learning, moving it from my waking mind into my unconscious, allowing me to play out my fears and effortlessly rehearsing a pattern of

69

movements that I am straining to achieve in real time. I am awash with it all, the blue pool, the craving for the open water, the waning of one body of knowledge and its usurpation by another.

But soon that also fades. After all, I am no longer just unlearning swimming. I am unlearning all of life, and how I used to live it. The pandemic brings a disordered, panicked unravelling. There is no time to reckon with it, only to act. That action forms a continuous chain across the whole of the next year, and more, and onwards. After a while I cannot remember how to do anything else. Like the swimming lessons, one form of knowing eventually takes over the other. For countless months, this urgent living was all that I was able to do.

And so when the old, familiar world came back again – slowly, haltingly, unsteady on its feet – I barely knew what to do with it. I unlearned it too well. The pool has reopened, and my friends have started to gather on the shore again. Possibility sparkles in the water once more.

But strangely, I am stranded. I can only stand at the water's edge, feeling reluctance floating in me. It makes no sense, but there it is: the water is no longer my domain. I've lost the salt that once felt so native in my blood. We meet again as strangers, unsure how to know each other.

There are moments when we must address our losses, without being fully conscious of what is lost. Somehow

I must find my way back into the water, if only because I remember there was once enchantment there, if only because I am not sure who I am without it. But the water is not to blame. It only shows the shape of the problem, having surged in to fill it. It is this negative space – this absence – that I need to understand.

THE TIDES

When I want to feel small, I go to the sea at its lowest ebb.

It's a skill peculiar to living near the coast, to have an innate sense of the rise and fall of the tide. When you walk there every day, you absorb its patterning, the way it changes shape across the week. Sometimes you can smell it, the salty reek of exposed seaweed carried inland by the wind or captured by a sudden fog. Sometimes you can hear it from a few blocks away, the slightly different quality of sound that rebounds when the water is present. When I've been away from the sea for a few days, I lose my sense of its rhythm, and I'm disoriented. It's like I've lost my clock.

I choose my time carefully to visit the shore. It's not the bulk of water that I crave, but its absence. Here in Whitstable, the sea retreats so far that it's barely visible, just acres of mud in its place. For many, this represents a peak of disappointment in the day, but not for me. I like to stand on the white part of the beach, where the ground beneath my feet is made mainly of crushed cockleshells, and to gaze at the sheer wall of the East Quay.

Specifically, I like to track the green line made by the high tide, metres above the bare seabed. I'm calculating the volume of water it must take to meet that line, savouring the gut feel of the vast brackish influx that comes twice a day. It's impossible, surely, but it happens like elemental clockwork, so quietly, so gently that you barely notice it. Spend half a day on the beach and you will know its soft power, the way it creeps up on you. I like to step down a little further on from the solid edge of the shore, into the place that will soon be inundated. The intertidal zone, that most liminal of spaces. I like to listen to the minute trickle of the water that remains. I like to imagine the sea far above my head.

Only occasionally do I remember that I am really watching the pull of the moon. The sun influences the tides, but only weakly; the moon's proximity to the earth, and her sheer scale, means that tides are gravity made visible. As the earth rotates, the sea reaches towards the moon, causing a high tide at the closest point. A simultaneous high tide rises at the opposite point on the globe, too, the farthest point from the moon. This one is a little more counter-intuitive: here, the moon does not exert enough gravity to pull the water inwards, and so the tide bulges in the other direction, freed from all constraints.

High tides happen when the moon is close, and when she is far away, and low tides occur in the spaces between.

The sun is just a helper, amplifying the moon, but it does have a very real influence on our perception of the tides. A day as we know it is twenty-four hours long, but the moon orbits the earth in twenty-four hours and fifty minutes. This means that from where we're standing, the tides shift by roughly an hour each day, moving restlessly through the mornings and afternoons, as if they are trying to escape us.

There are two giant waves travelling endlessly around the earth, and twice a day we see their full volume. We barely sense the scale of what is really happening, because we only ever witness it locally. We rarely stop to think that they join us to the entire planet, and to the space beyond it.

I am still trying to persuade myself to re-enter the sea. I am beginning to understand that it is not just a lost habit. The water is tempting, but its unsteadiness is not. That is because I, too, am unsteady. I've had Ménière's disease for about a decade now. Caused by an excess of fluid in the inner ear, it usually comes on like a migraine every couple of months, leaving me dizzy and nauseous. At those times, I have pills that curb its worst excesses, and I know that I'll need to spend a few days resting. This caused me a great deal of trouble when I was working full time – particularly as the attacks are triggered by stress and excessive screen time – but lately it's been merely inconvenient. I've adapted my life around it. I hate the episodes, but I've done all I can to ensure that they don't threaten my livelihood. With an incurable chronic illness, this is the best kind of a truce you can hope for.

Recently, though – since I had Covid – everything seems to have changed. The insides of my ears feel permanently swollen, and my eardrums are stretched to such a peak of sensitivity that I can feel the slamming of a door at the other side of a building. Waves of air pressure assail me, they boom and shift and flicker. My hearing is full of feedback, and I've lost my sense of direction. I can no longer tell where a sound comes from, and I'm often confused to hear Bert calling from another room, only to find him next to me. There are moments when I'm not sure I can hear at all if I can't see the speaker's mouth move. My ears are inflated. My entire head is a balloon, ready to burst. I begin to harbour fantasies – not uncommon in Ménière's sufferers, I'm told – that some benign physician might drill a hole in my head, allowing the air to hiss out. The thought itself, the unattainable fantasy, is a relief.

Worst of all is the dizziness. Years into this condition, I now know its various states. It doesn't always feel like the room spinning, although that happens often enough. Other times it seems like the house is off-level rather than me, all the furniture skewed. In this state, I will put a cup on a table and watch it slide off. I'm clumsy, even more than usual, and I begin to think that there should be a compensation scheme for people like me, whose crockery is smashed at an alarming rate and whose soft furnishings are all stained with spilt tea. If I go out, people tell me I'm walking at a slant, leaning sideways to correct some unseen force. The muscles in my back ache from holding me braced, and my face is often clenched with an effort that I don't even notice anymore.

At night, I frequently dream of Ménière's attacks so brutal that I'm pinned to the ground, unable to find my feet. It's extraordinary how my brain can conjure it, this absolute drunk feeling of my faculties dragged downwards. In these dreams, time slips and judders, and often I'm disoriented about where I am, and why and when. I wonder sometimes if this is my body feeling the full force of the vertigo while my brain is asleep and unable to intervene. Or maybe it's simply fear, imagining a dreaded future in which I lose more and more control, until all my lucidity is gone. What happens if I am helpless? What will become of me then?

It is not lost on me that this is a disease of too much water. I want to get back into the sea, but the sea isn't level enough anymore, and it is fundamentally too wet. It is no longer a break from the everyday. It is far too much

like the inside of my head. I am seasick, and I am homesick, and I am dizzy. I can't tell which one is the worst. I
miss the act of swimming. I miss the belief that my body
was capable, that it could endure, but then again, floating
no longer seems like much fun. I need a stable horizon
to which I can anchor myself. It's a matter of logic now,
rather than instinct. I have to take what I can get.

I also miss the community that came with it, the group
of women I used to swim with a few times a week, the way
we all felt brave together. I miss the ten minutes of intense
joyous chatter, the sense of release, of our stresses held
in the mesh of collective concern, even if for a few short
moments. I miss the wisdom of the group, the sense that I
could bring any problem there and have it gently probed
and understood, with solutions offered as the gifts of lived
experience. I miss the days when I could feel held by the
water and held by the people I swam with, all at once; and
when I felt useful enough to hold them in return.

But most of all, I miss the sense of worship that comes
when I get into the sea. I miss the feeling that I am entering a vast cathedral, and, rather than sitting in its dry
pews, that I am merging with it. I miss how when I feel
the pull of the tides, I am also feeling the pull of the whole
world, of the moon and the sun; that I am part of a chain
of interconnection that crosses galaxies.

★

My fantasy that I can somehow release the build-up of pressure in my head continues, and somewhere along the line, I realise that I am actually dreaming of trepanation.

The practice of boring a hole in the skull to reveal the thick membrane that encases the brain has a long and curious history. Archaeologists have found skulls with partially healed holes – suggesting that the subject survived the procedure – all over the world, and spanning millennia. Hippocrates and Galen both described the practice, and it continued in Europe well into the Renaissance period, where it was aimed at treating both mental and physical illness.

The small tribe of modern trepanners, who tend to cluster around the hippy fringes of the British aristocracy, believe that they are correcting a biological mistake. The fusing of the skull sutures at the end of childhood, they argue, restricts the brain's ability to pulsate freely and therefore suppresses the vitality, creativity and open-mindedness associated with being young. In 1995, after undergoing a DIY trepanation administered by her partner, Jenny Gathorne-Hardy wrote in the *Independent*: 'It was as though for years I'd been a puppet with my head hung down, and now the puppeteer had taken hold of my head string and was gently pulling it up again. I felt a clarity and gradual boosting of energy that didn't leave or diminish as time went by.' Trepanation, for this group, represents a resetting of the biological clock and even hints at eternal youth.

The reason for the earlier instances of trepanning are not known, although of course we speculate. It's clear that in some cases, fragments of the skull were removed after a traumatic injury, but that certainly wasn't universal. Some burr holes were made on healthy and even high-status individuals, men and women. There are theories linked to demonic possession, epilepsy and migraine, as well as spiritual questing or clarity. Did ancient people perform this rudimentary surgery to let something out or to let something in?

I begin to wonder if my own yearning for a hole in the head is a little bit of both. I want to release the pressure and clear the terrible fog that increasingly seems to cloud my mind. I'm also longing to open a window into which something might flow that currently seems beyond my reach. I don't mean it literally: I'm not in any way considering amateur cranial surgery. But I do understand the impulse behind it, that connection between head, mind and brain, and the sensation that my thoughts are packed in there like a baying crowd. If I could only find a way to liberate them, it seems to me that space would be made for the fragile voices I can't yet hear.

The psychologist Julian Jaynes thought hearing voices once came naturally to us. Whereas most of science assumed that we had always experienced consciousness in the same way, Jaynes thought that our ancestors' minds were very different to ours. In his 1976 book, *The Origin of Consciousness in the Breakdown of the Bicameral Mind*, he argues that our ability to introspect – to examine our conscious thoughts and feelings – arrived in relatively recent history, around the second millennium BCE. Before then, our mind was *bicameral*, two-chambered. 'At one time,' he says, 'human nature was split in two, an executive part called a god, and a follower part called a man.' We were not conscious in the way we now expect to be, able to isolate ideas, thoughts and feelings and to believe we generated them ourselves. Instead, we experienced thought as a series of auditory hallucinations, which we believed to be the voice of god. These voices told us what to do, and we lived under their direction. At the time of *The Iliad* and *The Epic of Gilgamesh*, we were all voice-hearers.

Jaynes asserts that the nature of our consciousness emerges from the language we use, and that we developed the language of the autonomous self only around four thousand years ago. Brains are 'plastic' organs – they modify their neural pathways according to how we want to use them – and so a different conceptualisation of what we are will determine the way that the brain develops. When we started to use metaphorical language, we

uploaded a new operating system, one that could uncon-
sciously imagine an 'I' that drew together our way of
perceiving the world into one stable person with agency.
We started to create our own life narratives in which we
were in control, and we stopped hearing the voice of god.

Jaynes's god is never an objective reality. He's never
talking about a supernatural being, but rather a messa-
ging system from one part of the brain to the other, which
seemed like the commanding voice of a more authorita-
tive being. God in this sense is the mode of communication
between the legislative and executive branches of your
self-government. We had no need for prayer as we now
know it, because the relationship was already face to face.
There was, says Jaynes, 'a matter-of-fact everyday relationship of god and man' with no need to make petitions.

It is, of course, a controversial opinion, developed not
from brain scans but from a close reading of classical literature. It is unsettling to imagine that the mind, our most
basic contact with being human, is not a stable phenomenon, and understanding the theory entails several leaps
of faith as we try to imagine that it is possible to think in an
entirely different way. On the other hand, there are some
ways in which the bicameral mind makes more sense to
me than the ill-fitting accounts I've been taught to believe
about myself. I often receive emotions and insights that
seem to arrive with no heredity in conscious thought, and

I have to undergo a process of tracing them backwards to understand where they came from. Intuition is a little like this, those gut feelings that are hard to interrogate through logic but which are compelling and often entirely correct. I relate to the theory as a writer who has never once consciously thought up an idea for a book or a story, but who instead seems to receive ideas whole, often in a dream. I don't have access to the part of me that invents. I just receive the blueprints and bustle around to make them work.

I feel a kind of yearning towards Jaynes's account of ancient prayer as a direct encounter, an ongoing conversation. There is a part of me that is still seeking this, I think. And like my ancestors, I could comfortably believe that the wisdom I channel comes from a greater mind than mine.

Amid all the time I am pinned to the sofa, unable to fix my eyes on anything, I think about this a lot: the absence I feel of that voice, that conversation. I had assumed that my sense of grinding to a halt must be the result of something I'd lost recently, something that had been present in my life, which now was absent. I had thought it would be as simple as identifying that thing and getting it back.

But now, with contemplation forced upon me, I realise I am groping past that, towards something I do not yet know, but which I know I need. It is a little like an unused instinct, the call of the wild felt in a domesticated animal like me. Perhaps I am struggling to assimilate all the changes that have patterned this earth over the last decade, but it strikes me forcibly that I am living in only one dimension. It's not just a matter of being confined to home. It's a whole existence that's constrained and over-reasoned, full of fear. This life I have made is too small. It doesn't allow enough in: enough ideas, enough beliefs, enough encounters with the exuberant magic of existence. I have been so keen to deny it, to veer deliberately towards the rational, to cling solely to the experiences that are directly observable by others. Only now, when everything is taken away, can I see what a folly this is.

I don't want that life anymore. I want what Julian Jaynes's ancients had: to be able to talk to God. Not in a personal sense, to a distant figure who is unfathomably wise, but to have a direct encounter with the flow of things, a communication without words. I want to let something break in me, some dam that has been shoring up this shamefully atavistic sense of the magic behind all things, the tingle of intelligence that was always waiting for me when I came to tap in. I want to feel that raw, elemental awe that my ancestors felt, rather than my tame, explained modern version. I want to prise open the confines of my skull and let in a flood of light and air and mystery. I want this time of change to change me. I want to absorb its might, its giant waves travelling around the planet. I want to retain what the quiet reveals, the small voices whose whispers can be heard only when everything falls silent.

We are a forgetful species, obsessed with the succession of tasks that hover over our days, and negligent of the grand celestial drama unfolding around us. And here I am, remembering.

PILGRIMAGE

Early Sunday morning, and the church bells are ringing as I wait by a bus stop in the village of Harbledown. I am not catching a bus, though. I am waiting for my friend Clare, who wants to take me on a very small pilgrimage.

The St Nicholas Hospital was founded just outside Canterbury in 1084, and was probably the first of its kind in England, a place where people with leprosy (now called Hansen's disease) could live together on the edges of society, in an almost monastic fashion. They paid their way by begging and saying prayers for the souls of their benefactors. The choice of location is similar to other leper hospitals, which were often on crossroads outside major cities, but there may have been another factor here: a natural spring, thought to have healing properties.

It is not entirely clear whether the spring came first and the hospital followed, or whether the spring was co-opted by the hospital to enhance its offer. Either way, it was renowned as a place to cure leprous ailments, and when Edward of Woodstock, the heir to the throne, visited the well and was cured of his leprosy, its reputation grew.

Edward drank the waters again in 1376 on his deathbed
– reputedly to cure syphilis this time – but to no avail.
Nevertheless, the well took on his soubriquet, and is now
the Black Prince Well.

Healing wells are scattered across the English landscape in surprising abundance – the historian James
Rattue lists over two hundred in my native county of
Kent alone. The vast majority, though, are forgotten.
Abandoned, overgrown, covered up, or derelict, they lie
invisible in the landscape, slowly seeping out centuries of
ritual significance. The Black Prince Well is barely known
among locals, but it is at least still maintained. It now
finds itself at the edge of a complex of retirement homes,
the grass around it carefully mowed. Elsewhere, it would
receive a steady stream of visitors. Here in Canterbury,
we have enough medieval grandeur to be complacent.

I'm not sure I would have found it at all if I'd come
alone. It is tented by an enormous briar rose with thick
branches covered in thorns. Clare pushes back the
boughs to reveal an arch of grey limestone whose worn
keystone is carved with the three-feathered insignia of
the Black Prince. There are steps down to a pool of dark
water about a foot deep, the heart-shaped petals of the
rose floating on its surface. Every now and then, a few
bubbles rise up lazily as the spring feeds in from below.

It is an extraordinary sight, this place where people

have come across the ages in the hope of healing. Its surround is worn like pumice, with the carved centre-pieces fitted in haphazardly, as though borrowed from somewhere else. It has the air of a place that has waited patiently for a long time for someone to come along and worship, and now it has me standing awkwardly before it, at a loss. It crackles with magic, but I have no template for how to behave around it, no tradition or culture that prepared me for this. There was once a chain of under-standing that stretched across generations, but that was broken long ago. All I have inherited is the forgetting.

'What do you do here?' I ask Clare.

'I go down the steps,' she says. 'I just spend time here.'

She ducks under the brambles and treads down to the water, and I look away, uncertain. Is this too intimate a moment for me to observe, or is this, after all, how we are supposed to learn how to interact with these places? I divert my attention to examining the golden starburst in the centre of every rose and running my hands over the winding trunk of an old silver birch that stands next to the well.

When Clare re-emerges, it's my turn. I kick off my shoes and crouch down to get underneath the briar. Neverthe-less, it catches at my back and pulls my raincoat right off.

'It's a guardian!' says Clare. 'It's looked after this well for a long time.'

I look up at the rose, which now vaults above my head. 'Please may I visit your well?' I ask. I'm not sure how it's supposed to reply, but I leave my jacket in its custody, in case it requires collateral to guarantee my good behaviour. The short passage down to the water is damp, with maidenhair fern growing from the cracks in its mortar. Just a few steps away from the path, I find myself in a very different kind of space, the sound of the outside world muffled, and my own movements echoing back from the stone and the water. The transition is immediate and unmistakable: here is a hierophany, a place imbued with layers and layers of human intent. The spring plays them back to me like a cassette tape, its meanings encoded in ways I don't fully understand. In the quiet, there is just the water and me, and we have nothing to do but make a reckoning with each other.

I let my toes touch the edge of the spring and reach down my fingers to disturb the floating petals. I can't resist tasting the water, which is clean and slightly mineral, and striping a little onto my forehead. What do I think I'm performing – some kind of baptism? I don't know. I suppose that pilgrims would once have drunk freely from this hallowed source, but my modern sensibilities warn me to trust only bottles and taps. I feel a little ashamed. Yet another failure of faith. Yet another half-hearted act of worship.

Others have been here in recent weeks. There is a cockleshell resting in the gap between two bricks, and at the bottom of the shifting water is something blue and gleaming. I roll up the legs of my jeans and step down into the basin, feeling the unsullied cold of the spring. Submerging my hand, I retrieve a solitaire cut from blue glass, a gemstone big enough to fill the palm of my hand. I don't want to interfere with the wish it represented, so I let it float back down to the bottom again. The well and its rituals have life in them yet.

I have been wondering how to speak to a God like mine – this idea that I have drawn from thin air, from my own unstable perceptions. I have reached the point in my life when I need the sense of contact with a consciousness wiser than my own, less frustrated and afraid. I want to be able to talk and to feel certain that someone is listening. But the belief itself wavers. Sometimes I believe that I believe. Sometimes even that is too much for me to assimilate. I feel foolish about the whole thing. I don't know how to do this.

Slowly and slyly it had crept into me, this conviction of . . . what? That something is there, something vast and wise and beautiful that pervades all of life. Something that is present, attentive, behind the everyday. A frequency of consciousness at the low end of the dial, amid the static. A stratum of experience waiting to be uncovered. It is the 'oceanic feeling' that puzzled Freud, 'a feeling of something limitless, unbounded' that existed in some people, but not in the father of psychoanalysis. Freud thought it was likely to be a function of the evolved mind, certainly not a perception of the numinous. I share his discomfort, but I can't agree. I have been trying to suppress the feeling for years. I kept telling myself that I was seeking a humanistic delight in the natural world, but that never felt quite like the truth. Slowly it expanded to become an uprising in me: fervent, persistent, seditious. It massed outside my walls, shouting and waving banners. I couldn't put it down.

When I try to understand what it is that I believe, I'm like a child caught in play. There is no solidity. Sensation gathers in my peripheral vision, but dissipates when I turn to look at it directly. It does not survive my scrutiny, any attempts to systematise or analyse. It is a different kind of belief, a different kind of feeling. It requires faith, and I have always been short on that.

My meditation practice asks me to soften into receptiveness. It has taught me to receive difficult thoughts in quiet and stillness, and to digest them before I rush to a response. But now that every element of my life feels passive, this feels passive, too. I need to talk. I need a repository for the dark little notions that skitter about my brain like biting insects. Preferably something that would cremate them entirely, but failing that, something that would offer a balm to soothe their stings. I want to learn to pray, but I don't know how to pray. I want to put my hands together, but I don't know what that would mean. I don't want intermediaries. I don't want interpretation. I want to speak plainly and directly to an entity that I can't quite perceive, and I don't have the language for that.

In the weeks that follow, the well takes up residence in my mind, as Clare told me it would. It seems to me to invite interaction: with its gnarled stone arch and the steps down to the spring, it ushers you in. It wants to be tended. But the well is also profoundly enigmatic, because that's where the invitation ends. Once you're there, you're on your own. It offers no clues for what to do, no liturgy or ceremony. At the bottom of those steps, you must confront your own yearning to make meaning. The water reflects only your troubled face. You are in fact the one who fills the well.

I often think that ritual gives us something to do with our hands rather than our heads, performing a set of actions that root us into our being again. Ritual is different from worship: a matter of instinct rather than construction, a gesture that lets us weave significance in the moment. It is so undemanding, so simple, almost passive. You follow the steps, and they take you down to find what you need.

At this point in time, ritual is exactly what I need. The world is unfurling all around me after too many seasons held unnaturally in bud, and as everyone surges outwards in some relief, I am still held in tight. I am enthralled by the reality of people again, that wonderful, terrifying, engulfing human noise that I've missed so much. My brain has forgotten how to manage, it seems. I keep stuttering off into silence, all the while wanting to go out and breathe it all in again.

We are just approaching Lammas. Arriving on 1 August, as the summer tips past its peak, Lammas is the first harvest festival of the year. It marks the moment when the grains are ripe in the field, and work begins to garner the fruits of the warm months before the cold sets in. Its name derives from the Anglo-Saxon for Loaf Mass, and although it's unclear how exactly it was celebrated (or whether it was celebrated at all – it could have just been a marker in the calendar), there is a living tradition of baking a loaf with the new flour and taking it to church for a blessing.

It strikes me that a Lammas loaf is a therapeutic project: an hour or so of working dough in the hands is a ritual all of its own. Lammas loaves can be plaited or shaped like human or animal figures, but I settle for a wheatsheaf loaf, formed from a hard dough enriched with a little butter. I knead it and let it rise, and then knock it back before dividing it in half. First I form the base of the loaf, the shape of a mushroom slice. Then I section off small pieces to roll a mass of thin stalks and torpedo-shaped wheat ears. Put together with a band around the middle, my creation is surprisingly handsome. It seems some of my angst has been absorbed into its very fabric through the pummelling of my hands. It's as though I've allowed a different part of my body to think for a while, alleviating the pressure on my brain. I think grimly that I might need to make quite a few loaves in the coming weeks. I add the traditional mouse to hide amid the stalks – a reminder of who will eat the grain if it is not harvested quickly – and let the bread prove again, then bake it. It emerges from the oven golden and glorious, and feels like my greatest achievement in a long time.

The next morning, I meet Clare at the well again. We have come prepared this time: I have cuttings from the grapevine that grows over my fence by the kitchen, and a bunch of garden mint. Clare has lavender and damask roses, and a handful of tiny pears, not yet ripe, from her tree. Wise now, we give the rambling rose an offering this time – an ox-eye daisy tucked between its thorns – and so we are allowed to keep our shirts on our backs as we tread down to the well. We arrange the vines and flowers over its stones and float herbs in its water. We use oyster shells to weigh down some crow feathers we found on the grass. I could invent a story about what each item meant, but it would not be true. We offer what we can find to the well. When we are finished, it is tended to, remembered.

We sit on the lawn and break the bread, eating it dipped in hot coffee from a flask. Then we each in turn spend time alone with the spring. The waters are scented with the last gasp of summer – mint and rose – and the crumbling stone looks proud in its dressing of leaves. I prop a piece of the Lammas bread against its arch, in the hope that some birds will find it. Either way, between the birds and us, the well is populated again. The two of us have woven enchantment, reconnecting this place to its old meanings and finding new ones of our own. It didn't take much. It was the simple work of willing hands, an act of listening, a commitment to seeing a place that had become invisible.

I realise, as I stand there with my feet in the water, that I don't need to ask the well for anything, not for a blessing or a wish, or for knowledge that I can't find myself. I just need to make contact with a place that holds a residue of hierophany, to feel the connection between myself and the many other lost souls who have come here, not knowing quite what to say. Rather than to say any prayer, I needed to take care of this place, to make a gesture towards an invisible continuity of yearning. The mysteries it holds are not revelations or miracles, but the flow of unknowing across the centuries, the connection of wanting to understand.

In this moment, it seems to me that talking to God does not require faith, but practice. It is a doing rather than a believing, an act of devotion reciprocated in the same way it is made: mutely, through the hands and the feet, the myriad attentions of the body.

CONGREGATION

I'm standing barefoot on Hartland Quay with a group of women I don't know, but who are nevertheless familiar. We are a tribe, all dressed in dryrobes and towelling ponchos, brightly coloured swimming caps and goggles. We nod in recognition and talk about our shared love of rescue dogs (mine is sulking at the top of the cliff, because she's not allowed on the beach), the chance that the weather will change tomorrow. The tide is far in and deep blue, a cloudless sky above it. My friend Jennie is just getting changed behind us. I want to get in before I can overthink it.

I'm nervous. I fear I'm about to lose face. The Hartland coast is jagged with outcrops of black basalt that ridge up through the seabed like the spines of lost creatures. I had always assumed it would be dangerous to swim here, but I'm assured it's the opposite: there are no currents dragging towards the harbour as in my native sea. The enclosed waters of the bay are safe and predictable on still days like this. It's the same cold, sapphire-blue Atlantic, but tamed a little. Nevertheless, I'm not used to the open water. I know I've lost strength, and certainly confidence. I'm just beginning to find a balance in my medication that means I'm not dizzy all the time, but the open water seems very big indeed for a wobbly person like me. I don't trust it, and I don't trust myself. I feel I've aged a decade in this last year.

Jennie – who is fond of telling me that she's old enough to be my mother, but does not seem to possess half my sense of fragility – is pulling on her neoprene socks and checking that her plaits are secure on top of her head. 'We're going to swim out to Life Rock,' she says, pointing at a spike of basalt in the middle of the bay.

'Is there a Death Rock?' I ask, mainly to conceal my nerves. Life Rock looks far away to me, and treacherously sharp. This is the famous wreckers' coast, full of snaring geology and hidden coves.

'Oh, I expect there's plenty of those,' she says.

I had already been on this very spot earlier today, but the tide was out and we hunted through rock pools for hermit crabs and the discarded homes of top shells, those tiny checkerboard cones that gleam with nacre. Bert had climbed Life Rock and stood at its summit, while I pretended not to be harbouring visions of his falling off. Now, with him safely eating chips on the hotel terrace above us, I can sense the geological formations that we clambered over this morning. Having absorbed the heat of the sun all day, they are radiating it back out again, creating warm seams in the water.

We breaststroke side by side, catching up after months apart. The others surge ahead, but we keep a steady pace, and Jennie says she's sorry for slowing me down. This is absolutely not the case, and I protest too much. I don't fully trust myself to reach our destination, but I'm willing to exhaust myself trying. I've missed her. We are not everyday friends, only swimming companions, and when she moved away to Hartland, I felt as though my swimming group fractured a little. That was before we were all thrown into the uncertainty of lockdown. Now it seems beyond repair. We're all out of the habit on one level or another.

The sea is much deeper than I'm used to, but so clear that I can see all the way down. I have stood on the quay in winter and watched vicious waves buffeting the beach, but today the surface is nearly flat. Instead, there's a swell, a big, undulating movement beneath the surface that gently lifts and lowers us. It's far more leisurely than I expected, far more possible. It's reassuring to have other swimmers in front of us. They make me feel safe, witnessed. We watch them disappear into the V-shaped channel of Life Rock, and soon we are there, too, close enough to touch the wrinkled stone. The gap forms a kind of pool in which swimmers are bobbing, rolled back and forth by the swell.

The effect is more pronounced in here, powerful but benign. There is something childlike about entering that dramatic space just to be thrown from side to side. I think I'm probably the youngest one here, but we are all at play, putting our faith in the sea's gentle mood, its choice, today, not to assert its authority. For now, it cradles us.

We swim back via the cliffs at the far side of the bay, chevrons of shale and sandstone that were formed, Jennie tells me, over three hundred million years ago. I think of the gargantuan forces that could make the land fold like that, the astonishing scope of those geological aeons, and I feel deliciously small. Here we are, swimming in deep time. We have let the sea show us a fragment of its power, and in return, we've shown it our power and our will and our sheer exuberant joy.

That night, when I lie in bed, I can still feel that swell rising and falling in me.

A part of me is always suspicious of groups. I am by nature a solitary animal. I like to do things my way, and in my own good time. I'm resistant to timetables and demands on my attention, and to the kind of politics that always seem to arise between adults who join clubs. I hate organised fun. Overall, I prefer to make my own ad hoc arrangements with a couple of close friends. But more and more, I crave being part of a congregation, a group of people with whom I can gather to reflect and contemplate, to hear the ways that others have solved this puzzling problem of existence. Most of all, I want them to hold me to account, to keep me on track, to urge me towards doing good. Holding spiritual beliefs on my own is lonely. I want to be part of a group that makes me return to ideas that bewilder and challenge me.

I realise that this is contradictory, but I do believe that congregations can be loose enough to hold people like me, those who will attend unreliably and prefer to lurk on the sidelines. But I'm not sure where I'd start. I've often considered joining one congregation or another just to feel the immersion in collective prayerfulness, that distinctive atmosphere created by many minds paying quiet attention together. Nowhere has ever seemed to fit. I've hovered over the schedule for the local Quakers, and I take an almost stalkerish interest in several Buddhist *sanghas* across the country. Last year I seriously considered an invitation to join a local pagan group. But in every case, I didn't ever take the final step: actually turning up, actually joining. Nothing seems to quite fit, certainly not any better than the churches I already know. Whatever I chose, I'd be making a partial commitment, leaning towards some ideas and silently bracketing others. At best, I'd be a wavering presence in the room. I don't want to insult these wonderful communities by treating their beliefs as a 'best fit'. This is not the same as choosing a political party to vote for. It's far too delicate, far too personal.

I'm also wary of stealing from traditions that don't speak to my own time and place, bending them out of shape and only partially understanding them. I've noticed how often we do that, cherry-picking the comforting parts of complex religious traditions – usually the aspects that tell us everything's okay – and ignoring the counterbalancing obligations, particularly those that involve careful introspection. There are some very good reasons for being selective in our spiritual beliefs: religions tend to be tainted with the worldly prejudices of those who minister them, and it's worthwhile sifting these out to find the gems of beautiful thought contained within them. But for those who, like me, only ever want to sift, there's a real risk of justifying our worst behaviour. I often see internet memes that tell us we are just as we are meant to be, God-made, and that leaves me deeply uneasy. I may not have a divine voice whispering in my ear to render it all clear, but I'm fairly certain that God – however you conceive of him or her – didn't plan for any of us to be racist. Every one of us has some kind of work to do. A spiritual practice that blankets us in the analgesic of self-acceptance is just a sticking plaster for our narcissism. Congregations – ones that are allowed to express diversity of thought – hold us to account.

I tend to think that God is not a person, but the sum total of all of us, across time. That only makes the imperative greater. We have a duty to witness the broad spectrum of humanity, rather than to defend our own corner of it. That is the work I crave: the sense of contact. The possibility that it might change me in ways that I can't predict. The possibility that I might one day do better.

The Zen Peacemaker Order is an organisation devoted to engaging with the darkest moments in human life. It was first imagined in 1994 by Sensei Bernie Glassman, who conceived of a spiritual framework through which members could not just think about the interconnectedness of all people, but experience it and seek to bring about change. The ZPO was founded on three tenets: Not-Knowing, Bearing Witness, and Taking Actions. Anyone can join their community, regardless of their beliefs or the level of engagement they're seeking. To take part, you only have to bring a willingness to engage with the process.

These three tenets drew me to the Zen Peacemakers: they're structured around enquiry rather than certainty, and they urge us towards informed change. Not-Knowing is the starting point, inviting practitioners to abandon their preconceived ideas and beliefs. Roshi Wendy

Egyoku Nakao describes Not-Knowing as experiencing 'a flash of openness or a sudden shift to being present in the moment', which allows us to drop the heavy baggage of our political views, our preconceptions and our opinions, and to fall back onto the direct observation of the here and now.

Next comes Bearing Witness, a commitment to noticing the world as it is presented to you, with curiosity and compassion. For the Zen Peacemakers, this often means resting attention on the parts of life that we'd prefer to push to the backs of our minds. Only then do you consider the final tenet, Taking Action. Zen Peacemakers do not simply watch and sit on their hands, but instead take their time to engage with a situation before launching into a response. The nature of that response is not defined. In some cases, the act of witnessing might be enough, and it might be all we can do. Other times, an action, big or small, may present itself spontaneously to us. Either way, we must not see this as linear, but should instead return to the state of not-knowing over and over again. Each round of observation brings us closer to understanding the true nature of reality.

The Zen Peacemakers are perhaps best known for their 'bearing witness retreats', which see members spending a week in sites of collective trauma, most famously in Auschwitz-Birkenau, but also in Jerusalem, among homeless people in cities across the world, and with the Native American Lakota community in South Dakota. Bernie Glassman used the word *plunging* to describe the experience of these retreats. Participants immerse themselves in an environment full of painful truths, setting aside their assumptions and preconceptions. These are places that often hold personal significance for those who attend, speaking to shameful or tragic family histories. The retreats reconnect people with the humanity of what happened, the way that our own bodies know the terrible things that are done to others. The retreats are also an act of healing, ending with a ceremony aimed at soothing the unrested souls who linger at sites of mass suffering.

Inevitably, the pandemic meant that in-person retreats were not possible for a time, but that opened up a chance for me to attend an online retreat instead, a 'deep dive' into race in America that took place over a long weekend. I was apprehensive when I logged into Zoom on a Friday afternoon, worried that my presence might be intrusive or inappropriate. As the session began, though, I realised that I would be challenged in an entirely different way. With my attention shattered, the prospect of being present for three hours flickered anxiously within me. I doubted that I could be still and listen for so long. Even in the opening moments, in which we were urged to sit in our discomfort and try not to look away, I could feel my hands itching to do something while I watched. I felt guilty about taking time away from the rest of the house for this; I felt lazy and unproductive. I wondered if I could blank my screen, carry my laptop into the kitchen, and cook while the retreat rolled on.

But of course that would make it like everything else in this contemporary life: one of many simultaneous flows of information with which we half connect. To make this an act of worship – to make a connection with the other people gazing down this digital channel – I needed to be wholly there. I thought about how, in church, there's nowhere to hide. The hard pews won't even let you daydream. You have no choice but to give the service all your attention. I needed to do the same here, even though I wasn't being kept in line by disapproving eyes. I fetched matches from the drawer in the hall and lit a candle on my desk and then, to occupy my hands, I picked up a round stone that rests by my monitor and held it in my hands. Its weight, its gravity, helped me to sit still.

That weekend, we listened to many different voices giving their first-hand accounts of racism, taking us through the terrible history of slavery, lynchings and police brutality towards Black bodies. The sitting-still part became even less easy. It felt like waiting passively for blows to land. But I noticed something in that stillness. The act of witnessing changed a topic I thought I already knew.

Without the ability to question or console or solve or apologise, I lost all the tools that would usually smooth over the ideas in my mind. I had to find a new engagement, and I heard more this time around than I'd ever heard before. Witnessing made the past events more complex and the present ones more pressing. I didn't actually want to look away. I couldn't.

At the end of each day, we broke off into small groups for a key part of the Zen Peacemakers' practice, the Way of Council. Derived from Native American tradition, this is a reflective meeting that aims to deepen the experience of witnessing. Only one person speaks at a time, and all are urged to speak from the heart, being spontaneous in what they choose to share and keeping it as concise as possible. Everyone else is asked to listen without analysing or discussing, and this even includes expressing approval. You speak as truly as you can and receive only attentiveness.

The confidentiality of the group is absolute, and for that reason I will say only that the council sessions were a welcome end to each day, helping me to sort through tangled feelings and to hear the unvarnished responses of my companions. For much of the time, we sat in silence, waiting to see if words would form in our mouths. I reflected that I knew these American examples of white supremacy better than I knew the stories from my own country; I had a responsibility to cast my witness closer to home. I was back to knowing nothing again, or at least knowing very little.

I was moved most of all by the gentle compassion of a community that doesn't seek to fill contemplative space with words, that is willing to trust individual feelings and to sit with conflict and doubt. It was rare and beautiful to be part of creating that ecology. On the third day, we were urged to remember our own self-care before we began, to pay attention to the physical landing this knowledge had made in us. I was slightly ashamed to be in need of that. At points I could feel my capacity to witness running dry, particularly the cases of Black children my son's age being murdered, but also those of white children brought along to watch the lynchings. Both struck me as acts of devastating violence that could not do anything but ricochet through generations. But strangely, when some of the speakers expressed breathtaking levels of forgiveness and hope, I found it equally hard to stay present. It was beyond my capacity for understanding. I could see how much I had left to learn about the possibility of redemption.

We had travelled through not knowing and bearing witness. The weekend ended with a step towards taking action. We took part in a Gates of Sweet Nectar ceremony, a process of chanting and song that symbolically feeds the hungry ghosts of Buddhist scripture. These are the souls of people who died sudden or violent deaths, or who are forgotten by their descendants. They have tiny mouths and huge stomachs, so they are eternally hungry. In Chinese tradition, they are left food and drink at harvest time. Here, we take a more symbolic approach. Chanting the words of the Krishna Das song 'Calling Out to Hungry Hearts', we invite them to 'Gather round and share this meal / Your joy and your sorrow / I make it mine.'

To me, these ghosts are both real and not real, a projection willingly given solid form. The most I can do for people whose suffering happened long ago is to offer my entirely impractical concern. I don't honestly believe that it helps them, but it's an assertion of our interconnection. It cements an intent to care in the present day, a promise made collectively before my congregation. I witness, and I am in turn witnessed, and between the two lies an obligation to do better in the future. The exact nature of that doing is left unnervingly undefined. That bit is up to me. It is the beginning of a practice that is supposed to last a lifetime, to change and respond, to be founded on repeated listening, repeated learning, repeated action. It is supposed to sift into me like water working through strata.

But there's a final change that my weekend with the Zen Peacemakers makes in me, one that seeps into my life more than anything else I absorbed in those hours: I learn to place my hands together in prayer, in greeting, in a bow of respect and in a moment of contemplation. It is quite unlike the gesture of prayer I learned at school. It is fluid, agile, a way of closing a bodily loop. It's internal and external all at once, a hit of contact, just like putting my feet on the floor. It connects a current that can flow in many directions. I am allowed it, I realise. I am allowed to make what I want of my own two hands. The gesture is mine to offer, and I trust that it will be understood by the people who share my prayerfulness.

My favourite childhood memory – the one I often fetch up just to roll around in my mind and savour – is swimming in the sea with my grandad. He would stand knee-deep in the shallows, scoop me up in his enormous hands, and throw me head first into the waves. I would let the force of the water tumble me over until I couldn't tell which way was up, then find my feet again and run back to him for more. Over and over, for what seemed like a blissful eternity, we would play together, wordlessly, inexhaustibly.

When I asked him about it years later, he told me that he'd always been afraid to swim himself, but that he wanted it for me – to feed my insatiable desire for water. He remembered standing there, shivering, his arms aching with the strain, but I would be back, wanting one more splash, one more chance to lose myself again. He didn't want to say no, so he never once let on. I find it hard to imagine him being afraid of anything, so it must have worked. He gave me everything I needed, then and now: the simple faith in water, the thrill of pitching forwards into the unknown, the knowledge that wonder can be transferred through the skin. But most of all, he showed me what it was to be held by other hands, to be thrown into uncertainty, and to know I would be caught again. The congregation of the Zen Peacemakers did the same.

It's one of the many reasons I'm glad to be back in the water: I know of nothing else that takes me quite so absolutely to the edge and delivers me safely back again, providing I show it enough respect. But I have not returned to my swimming lessons. Perhaps that's because I had already learned enough to get by, and perhaps also because my ears are better off staying above the surface these days. But most of all, after a year on dry land, I got a little more perspective. The pool was too confined for me. It had no flow. I do not swim to travel through the water, to merely accumulate metres and miles. I swim to enter into the midst of something that joins me to everything, everywhere, in all time.

When I learned about the water cycle in school, it seemed straightforward: a matter of evaporation, rain,

rivers and seas. But only recently did I begin to understand what that preserved: the water endures, sublimating
between states, becoming brackish, being cleansed, infil-
trating into the soil. Between water and our bodies there
is effortless communication, both engaged in an endless
saturated exchange.

I have only ever wanted to explore that relationship,
to play in the space in which we're all immersed. I have
begun to find other ways to meet water, for those times
when I am too unsteady to float. After tasting the water
in the well, I've started to drink from all the streams and
lakes I pass through, each place I walk and each place
I swim. I've bought a portable water filter that promis-
es to secure me against anything that would disturb my
feeble twenty-first-century gut – bacteria, viruses, chemical residue. It's smaller than the water bottle I used to
carry, and so much lighter. Now when I'm thirsty, I stop
by a stream, dip in my cup, plunge the filter, and slake
my thirst at that particular place. I like to think that the
water in each location tastes subtly different, but it's hard
to compare. What I do know is that it's different from
water that I've carried from home and treated with chlorine to make it safe, water that has gone warm and stale
in my bag over the day. Stream water is delicate. It tastes
of clarity. When I drink it, I feel like I'm imbibing the
deep layers of rock beneath my feet and the clouds above.

But I am also swallowing those times, long past, when I could inhabit the same sea as my grandad.

It is the same water, then and now. It is the same sea that flows across the whole world. It is just one of the ways in which we're all connected.

FIRE

THE NIGHT THE STARS FELL

In the early hours of 13 November 1833, those who were awake shared an extraordinary sight. According to the *New York Evening Post*, it seemed that 'the cape of heaven was raining down a shower of fire' over the eastern states of America. Shooting stars came in such density that 'the whole firmament appeared to be in motion with them, as if the planets and constellations were falling from their places'.

In the time before electric light, night-wakers were well used to seeing meteors scuttling across the heavens, but this was different. The black bowl of the sky was suddenly full of sparks, a thousand at a time, all drawing silvery lines like the ribs of a celestial umbrella. Never before had anyone seen the sky's arc so clearly described: it was as though a curtain had been drawn back to reveal the truth – known, but never really understood – that the earth is a ball floating through the vastness of space, and that we, its motion-sick citizens, are only ever spectators of this grand planetary drama.

Witnesses experienced a bombardment of light so

intense and tangible that they fully expected their houses to catch fire. The stars did not appear to be falling in some dark, abstract space, but right above the heads of the folk who watched, and cowered, and prayed. The largest of the sparks flashed like lightning and were as big and bright as Venus. Some claimed they were bigger still, able to eclipse the moon. A few reports said they crackled and hissed; others described explosions like silent fireworks. Many thought they shimmered with prismatic colour. Somehow, despite the intensity with which all watched the meteors, nobody could quite agree on their exact form.

By 5 a.m. the stars were fading, and they vanished altogether with the arrival of the sun. 'Early risers find almost every day some cause for exulting over those who lie-a-bed till breakfast time,' wrote the *Philadelphia Chronicle*. 'We have never known them so triumphant as to-day.'

Commentators wasted little time in trying to make sense of what had taken place on that cold, clear night. From Nova Scotia to Florida, amateur astronomers and newspaper correspondents groped for words to describe what they saw, and were as likely to find poetry as scientific accuracy. The *Baltimore Patriot* called the moment 'one of the most grand and alarming spectacles which ever beamed into the eye of man', and counted stars 'as numerous as ever I saw flakes of snow or drops of rain in the midst of a storm'. To the editor of the *Commercial Advertiser* in Kingston, Jamaica, the shower was reminiscent of 'shoals of dolphins sporting and minutely rising from the ocean'. Witnesses struggled to quantify the sparks that were visible during this time, but the most reliable guess came from a physicist called Joseph Henry, who estimated that twenty points of light per second were appearing in the sky, which tallied to seventy-two thousand per hour. Some believe the number was even higher.

The following day, the *New York Evening Post* stated rather condescendingly that the 'atmospheric phenomenon . . . excited vague apprehensions in the minds of ignorant persons', and noted that 'an unusually small number of country people attended the market that morning'. For some, the apprehensions were more than vague. *The Old Countryman*, a generally humorous weekly paper in North Carolina with a considerable circulation, carried an editorial letter full of fire and brimstone. 'We pronounce the Raining Fire which we saw on Wednesday morning last an awful Type—a sure Forerunner—a merciful SIGN of that great and dreadful Day which the inhabitants of the Earth will witness when the SIXTH SEAL SHALL BE OPENED! Many things occurring on the earth tend to convince us that we are in the "LATTER DAYS".'

Prophecies aside, the lights of science had yet to understand the source of such a celestial display. It was clear to astronomers that meteors were not literally falling stars, but their actual nature remained vague. The meteor (meaning simply 'atmospheric phenomenon') had yet to take solid form in the scientific imagination and was thought to bear more relation to a streak of lightning or an efflorescence of the Northern Lights than to anything that fell from space.

It would take several decades – and the slow unfolding of a thirty-three-year cycle – for astronomers to understand the true nature of the Leonid meteor showers that happen each November. But whether this starfall brought about a sudden awareness of the grand scale of the universe, an urgent call to the rigorous pursuit of the scientific method, or a renewed respect for the wrathful might of God, here was enchantment, falling like rain on expectant rooftops, demanding attention and making the humans below wonder about the relatedness of all things, the strange machinations of the universe.

☾

Nostalgia always seemed to be the domain of other people until one night it hit me hard.

Attending the opening of a friend's play, we drive down to Gravesend, past all the places I knew as a child: across Echo Square, where my mother worked in a bakery; past

Woodlands Park, where I used to play; down the High Street with its weatherboarded shops and grand market hall like a Greek temple. They seemed so big back then, so vital to the smooth running of the universe, but of course they were small all along. Everywhere is. That particular night, nostalgia gathered around them for me like residual magic, like hierophany. I went down to the river and watched it run, broad and black, through the town. I saw the red lights on the chimney stacks a little further along the opposite shore.

During the intermission, I told a man I knew that I used to live here. 'This is where I'm from,' I said. It was no great claim to make, but I wanted to make it all the same, to show how this place could be loved.

'Do you still have family here?' he asked.

And I had to think for a while, running through all the people who might be mine. Some dead, some moved away. 'No,' I said, surprised at this new knowledge. 'No, I don't think I do.'

I hadn't noticed when that last tie had been cut. Is that how nostalgia is made: a yearning for somewhere you no longer want to be, but which seems, in an instant, perfect? Or perhaps *perfectible* is a better word, a place that you could restore to the glories you still see in it, if only it would let you. If I had my way, I would reinstate the old Army & Navy department store, all the way down to the smell

123

of perfume around the entrance doors, and the speckled Formica in the ladies' toilet, and especially – especially – the rigid set of the women's hairstyles, and their headscarves and the belted rain macs they all wore. I would bring back the old cinema in a fug of cigarette smoke, showing *Ghostbusters* and *E.T.*, and I would restore, most of all, the burnt-milk smell of the café where my mother worked on Saturday mornings, and the faux-leather menus, and the way she would reach into her apron to pull out her notepad for my Crusha lime milkshake, just like she did for everyone else.

On the way home, I ask H if he could drive us past my grandparents' old house, taking the long way back to the motorway. It goes by in a flash, the sloped lawn rising up to an arched front door, still painted white. I wonder if the new owners polish the step like my grandma used to. But what it ushers back, most of all, is the memory of standing on that step and watching a house on fire a little further along the road. Of all the neighbours out, shielding their eyes to get a better look, and calling over hedges to share what little they knew: the old forge, they thought, but they couldn't see for all the fire engines. Everyone was there, watching, speculating, marvelling at how high the flames could go, how suddenly and completely it could all happen. The inhabitants were safe. It was just the building burning, one of the oldest in the village, a wooden frame on a warm night. In a quiet place where nothing much happened, this was a spectacle worth witnessing, pulling us all out together in the dark.

When I get home, I search the internet for an account of the fire, for some kind of record that would place that night – and therefore me, standing barefoot in my nightdress – in time. But there is nothing, not a single mention of that fire in all the pages of text about one tiny village in north-west Kent. I can no longer contact any-one who was there, and it seems that I am the only one left, treasuring the uncanny sense I had that night that something had happened to us, as a collective, some-thing that was of lasting importance. I am reminded of the Czeslaw Milosz poem 'Encounter', which recalls a simple moment, far back in time, when a companion pointed out a hare that ran out in front of his wagon as he rode through the countryside at dawn. 'Oh my love,' he writes, 'where are they, where are they going / The flash of a hand, streak of movement, rustle of pebbles? / I ask not out of sorrow, but in wonder.'

In summer months, I am in the business of catching moths. Where there is a lit bulb and an open window, I am there, too, cupping my hands around a fluttering form that's determined to hurl itself against the light. Both H and Bert are afraid of them – they are too quick, too intent. I don't think they mean to menace us, it's just that we're invisible to them, a thing of such scale that we're beyond perception. I will not have them batted with a newspaper, so I clamber over the kitchen table and balance on the backs of chairs to reach them before setting them loose into the night. It is a thankless task, because soon they are back again, bumping against the glass. It must be such a bafflement to them, this invisible barrier between desire and possibility.

We are more moth than we know: small, frustrated, capable of only tickling a world that we wish would feel our heft. We share that attraction towards the brightest object in our field of view, an equal fascination with candles and conflagrations. We sense the danger, but we can't look away. In fact we are drawn to circle it endlessly, getting closer and closer until it consumes us. Even when we think the sky might be falling, we stay to watch. It is elemental to us, this alertness, this panicked, flitting attention.

Fire is the shadow side of enchantment, the dark, gleaming sorcery from which we can't tear our gaze. It shows us the wild danger that still resides in nature, the power it retains to devour and destroy. It is impolite, contagious, capable of catching from house to house while we stand helpless. It licks our palms like a moth in cupped hands.

We have not understood this earth's full potency until we have recognised fire.

Too often, we have allowed ourselves to believe that we can live whole lives in the absence of suffering. We are told that uniform happiness is the only desirable experience. But this in itself is a disenchantment. Fire brings us back into contact with the cycle of life, with the limits of our control, and with the full spectrum of human feeling. It teaches us hard lessons and burns through our fragile illusions. Without it, we are living only a surface existence, a shallow terrain. We must assimilate fire to become whole again.

BURNING BOOKS

The chaos of lockdown feels far away now, and the sense of existential threat has receded, but I am still unable to read. Reading is the whole of me, the foundation upon which I rest, and these days I cannot do it. It is a dirty secret that I must keep, an ugly act of faithlessness in an author. I do not want to read. I cannot read. I cannot shepherd my attention towards a page of text and take in any words. I cannot complete a whole chapter without my consciousness excusing itself and quietly retreating into an inner sanctum to which I have no access. I cannot sit still. I cannot concentrate. Surely this is some kind of a malady for which there ought to be a cure?

This disconcerting outage hits fiction worst of all. I can browse through scraps of non-fiction, an article here and there. But novels: no. I have nothing for them. I am entirely uninterested in stories that didn't happen, in the interior lives of people who don't exist. I am overtaken by apathy. I know that this is a fault in me rather than in any book. But it is tangible, this cynicism, this turning away. I cannot get past it.

My lack of reading is a furtive thing, a fugitive state of being that I must not show to the people who know me. I feel disordered by it, the familiar world sliding out from my grasp. It is not as though I'm doing something else instead. I have not transferred my allegiance to Netflix. I am just not reading. There is a gaping void where I used to rest my mind.

I have begun to notice this malady in other people, too. I have been asking, slyly, for recommendations that would rekindle my passion, and nobody seems to know. Those literary friends of mine – those other readers, my people, who usually fizz with excitement about one book or another – are drawing a blank. 'What have you read that's good lately?' I ask. They shrug. They prevaricate. They say that such-and-such was okay, but they didn't really love it. They ask if I can suggest something in return. I cannot.

It seems to me that it perpetuates itself, this exchange of nothing. Behind it is an existential exhaustion, the sickness, the fear, the lockdowns, the stretching of the human mind past its capacity to manage. We have been running on empty for so long that we've lost the urge to refuel. We have spent so long anxiously scanning the news that we are now in a fixed state of objectless checking. This is our reading matter now. We are not looking for anything, we are just looking. It seems that if we stop looking, something terrible could happen. Looking is our magical thinking. It used to feel protective, but now it's turned dark. Now, if we don't check, if we don't perpetually look over our shoulder, we suspect we might bring about disaster. The last thing propping up the sky is our eternal vigilance.

When I think back now to how I learned to read, I do not think of those sticky childhood days, running my finger over large print. I think, instead, of my first week at university, when I was sent to meet my Director of Studies, and I travelled over to a college at the far side of town on my new bicycle, a birthday present in tribute to my new life. Wiping the sweat from my forehead – generated more by panic at navigating an unfamiliar network of paths than by exertion – I undertook the new and unfamiliar routine of D-lock and key, a plastic bag over the saddle in case of rain. Then I presented myself, falteringly, to the Porters' Lodge and was directed across two quads to a ground-floor office.

What I found there surprised me. I had not, in the first place, expected the room itself to be quite so beautiful, with French doors opening out onto a sunlit terrace draped in wisteria. The woman who opened the door was friendly and helpful, but at the same time naked- ly clever in a way that I had never yet encountered. As we talked, she exuded entitlement to seriousness and a simple acceptance of intellectual work that made her an exotic bird in my eyes, rare and fascinating. I didn't know it was possible to want to be this.

But most of all, I could not believe how many books were in that room. We were not, to the best of my knowledge, in a library, but I thought that perhaps they might be there on loan. Maybe the college owned so many that they distributed books throughout all the studies on campus, an arrangement that no doubt delighted the scholars. But no. That didn't make sense. I could see, already, that the titles all clustered around her research interests: social policy, economics, feminism. I had to ask.

'Are they yours?'

She gazed at them mildly for a few moments. 'Yes,' she said. 'All mine.'

'Have you read them all?'

'Of course,' she said. 'No use just owning them.'

There it all was: a whole galaxy of knowledge on those shelves. And not just there, either. It was there in the college library and the department library, in the giant University Library that was supposed to hold every single book in copyright. I had been to libraries before, but not like these. Everything was laid out, waiting for me. I wanted to assimilate all of it. I wanted, one day, to own a set of shelves like these.

But somehow I could not take it in. The reading skills I had – the blunt instruments of letters and words – were not equal to this task. It turns out that I had done only the palest part of reading before, racing through literary paperbacks and assimilating textbooks to populate exam papers at the end of each year. Here was a different kind of reading: disciplined, complex, unfathomable. Books that had to be assigned, searched for in long drawers of index cards, located on a shelf, and then, somehow, read and understood. This was the impossible part, because each book was nearly impenetrable, texts so dense with learning that they felt like intellectual black holes, informational molasses. Every single paragraph, every single sentence, depended on a backlog of knowledge to support my understanding. I could barely break in.

I would seat myself in one library or another, open the correct page, and then feel the words repel my eager eyes. I was rain, and they were waterproof. Who was I to come to them, this girl who didn't even know that this kind of knowing existed, who had never considered that she might be unequal to the task of taking it all in. Feeling stupid, I did a stupid thing. I stopped going to lectures. I stopped picking up reading lists. I found that it was easy enough to evade assignments and supervisions if only I kept a low profile. I was homesick, anyway. I was certain that this place wasn't for me. I thought I might achieve my leaving passively, and without anyone feeling too disappointed.

At some point, somewhere, I suppose there were missing marks in a register. I wasn't quite so invisible as I'd hoped. When it all caught up with me, my more usual levels of conscientiousness kicked in. I could not affect nonchalance, because I was absolutely not nonchalant. I was not working because I couldn't bear to turn in anything that so clearly revealed my imperfection.

Soon I washed up in that book-lined study all over again, a little more bedraggled. My Director of Studies turned her chair to face me, crumpling the pile of unmarked essays that were scattered at her feet.

'So,' she said, 'how is everything going?'

It was a loaded question, and I didn't want to answer it, so instead I blurted out the thought that was at the front of my mind. 'Everywhere I've been this week has set on fire.'

It was true, or true enough to feel real. I had spent Saturday afternoon shopping with a friend, and seen later on the news that a fire had broken out in one of the stores. The next day, driving out of a village where we'd stopped for lunch, I saw a curl of smoke rising from one of the fields, and later heard that it was an act of vandalism that had stopped the traffic for hours. And, well, here I was, having nearly burned down everything I'd worked so hard to achieve. That was surely something worth mentioning.

I was used to being scolded for abrupt changes of subject or for flippant comments, but the professor didn't do that. She thought for a moment and then said, 'You should pay attention when things like that happen. It might mean something.'

And it did, then and now. I no longer see myself as the girl who is so innately destructive that she might leave a trail of charred earth in her wake, but I do know that I am on first-name terms with burning, with blazing high and burning out. Here I am, back in that cycle of fuel, of conflagration, and of scorched earth. The loss that it brings – the complete collapse of self – is always agonising, but there's something I secretly like about it, too. After all, the bare ground invites a new kindling. To have nothing to lose, you have to first lose everything.

Once I had realised my talent for fire, I could allow myself to start all over again. My index finger returned to sweep over the lines in an effort to hold my eye steady. The slow chanting of syllables was back from childhood, too, sometimes even whispered aloud. I had to loop many times over each paragraph in an effort to understand. It was hard. I had fallen behind and was fighting my way back to meet everyone else. I didn't yet know, at that age, how to know nothing. I knew only how to pretend

I knew everything. It was a relief to admit that I was fallible. This humbling was like water poured over fire. I started from scratch, and it was surprisingly enjoyable to do so.

Perhaps I shouldn't fear this present-day burnout after all. It shows me only that I'm ready to be made again. How have I allowed this great pleasure in my life – the act of sitting quietly with a book and drinking in its words – to become so heavy, so freighted with obligation? Somewhere along the line, I lost the sense of playfulness that drew me towards it in the first place. No wonder my reading went on strike.

I always thought that my future self would have ranks of books like my professor, all of them read and understood, an achievement in the past tense that proved I had become something. I now see that this was not what she showed me. She offered me instead the act of knowing, rather than the static fact of the known, a lifetime of enquiry. I don't want to sit like a brooding hen on the nest of my past achievements. I want to keep on going deep into the uncertain act of making, to see the unknown world stretch out before me and to devote myself to exploring it.

So I begin again, just as I have before. I have learned to be grateful for these losses, painful and disorienting as they are. They make me small again. The next world is so tantalising, lying across a million unread pages, and in which I am nothing, nobody, new.

DEEP PLAY

I am six years old, and everyone else has a video recorder and a stack of films recorded from the TV to keep them company. But I do not, because I live at my grandparents' house, and they still rent their television. They have even chosen one that looks like a wooden cabinet, with a sliding door over the screen so that you can sometimes pretend that you don't have a television at all. A video is out of the question.

All the kids at school seem to be able to quote lines from Disney films, and know the words to all the songs in *The Water Babies*, but I do not, so I can't join in. What I have instead is two issues of *Story Teller*, a children's magazine with fairy tales that are read aloud on an accompanying tape. It has full-colour illustrations, and celebrity narrators whose status is entirely lost on me. This does not stop it from being my heart's desire. It seems to me that everyone else has the whole set, including the binders and the plastic suitcase for the tapes, but that kind of expenditure is not possible in my house. Two issues are probably enough anyway, because I am only obsessed with one story.

It is the first one in issue 26, which is lucky, because I keep on rewinding the tape. There is the annoying jingle that opens every recording, and then the clear, certain announcement: 'The Goblin Rat.' A gong sounds. A flute plays a pentatonic scale. A ping when you need to turn the page. The story tells of a boy born to a farming family who is too weak for physical labour, so his father takes him to the local temple to become a monk. The boy is clever and keen to learn, but he has one flaw: he can't resist drawing cats wherever he goes. After drawing cats all over the screens in the temple, he is cast out of the monastery and given some final words of advice by the abbot: 'At night, avoid large places. Keep to small.'

The story is a Japanese fairy tale, thought to be a mythology of the fifteenth-century artist Sesshū Tōyō. It was brought to the West by Lafcadio Hearn, an American who became a renowned collector of Japanese folklore after emigrating and marrying there. His collection, *Japanese Fairy Tales*, was published in 1898, and contained the story of 'The Boy Who Drew Cats'. It is apparently not terribly faithful to the original, with the contrast on its phantasmagoric elements tuned high. But it is nevertheless a striking tale, particularly for any child who is quiet and strange, prone to developing obsessions that infuriate the adults around them.

Journeying away from his monastery, the boy is drawn

towards a remote temple with blazing lanterns that seem to kindle his hopes that he can join this community instead, even if only as a cleaner. But he is unaware that the lanterns are known locally as the devil's lights, lit to tempt guileless travellers to their death. The temple is long abandoned and is populated only by a demon rat that has slain any warrior brave enough to confront it.

Finding the temple empty, the boy cannot resist falling into his old habit, taking out his ink brush and sketching cats all over the temple screens. Then, exhausted by his journey, he settles down to sleep, only remembering the abbot's words in his last drowsing moments. He rouses himself just enough to crawl into a cabinet, close the door, and fall asleep. He is awoken in the night by the sounds of scratching and hissing and screeching, and the walls of the temple shake with the fury of whatever is going on outside his door. Eventually, all falls silent, but it is not until first light that the boy summons up the courage to step outside. There, he finds the corpse of a giant rat, lying in a pool of its own blood. And his cats have changed. They still languish in loose brushstrokes across the walls of the temple, but now their mouths are smeared with blood.

In the traditional telling of the story, the boy becomes an abbot. In Lafcadio Hearn's rendition, he becomes an artist. Different aspirations for different times. Either way, to achieve the status he deserves, the boy has to undertake an act of humility, choosing a small space over the grand temple. The disobedient child listens to his master and saves himself in the process. But I don't think that's the only act of humility in the story. It seems to me that the boy's true submission is to his cats. His desire to paint them is elemental, a force of nature that ought not to be curtailed. His art burgeons out of him like a spring, regardless of temporal authority, the human vanity for buildings. He never seems more than a conduit here, painting cats because that is simply what he does. He is the brush. He is the ink. The cats are creating themselves. When the time comes, they save him.

'The Boy Who Painted Cats' describes a particular kind of fire: the necessary fire, the fire that burns clear in us, the fire that is too easily ignored. This surely is another enchanted space.

☽

I have started to walk the dog on Holly Hill, a short drive inland from my house. I find that a climb settles my mind like nothing else, and it's full of sights to absorb my stray attention, offering distant views over the estuary. I love the way that mushrooms seem to pop up all over this wood, scaling every tree and rising delicately through the leaf mulch. Occasionally I've found the turquoise-stained wood that betrays the presence of green elf cups there.

But lately I've been looking for something else. A couple of different friends have told me that there's a ruined folly at the very top of the hill, and it's marked on my map, too, as *tower*. This should be a simple enough mission: finding a tower at the top of a hill. But the strange thing is, I can't find it. I've looked several times now. The first time, I took Bert, and we circled the hill half a dozen times, at one point accidentally trespassing on someone's land. Another time, I went alone and followed every single tiny path, ranging all over the woodland. Nothing. I have printed out directions from someone who knows the place well, and still they seem to fox me. I feel as though the tower is deliberately eluding me, appearing for some people but not for me. Perhaps, like Baba Yaga's cottage, it has risen up on chicken legs and stalked to another part of the Kent countryside. Either way, it has begun to feel like a quest.

I have started to look up the meaning of place names recently. It is perhaps an interest that awakens in you as you age, this enthusiasm for peering back through time to find lost meaning. It started when I noticed that the River Dart where I holiday in Devon and the River Darent near my childhood home both have derivations of the same Celtic name, meaning 'river where oak trees grow'. There's a lot contained in those short names: an ancient understanding of the landscape, a contested cultural history (not everyone agrees that there were ever Celts in Kent), and a link between two places that I know and love. In a time when I am unable to concentrate on novels, this unfolds the same kind of information for me as a book once did, these networks of satisfying ideas that speak to one another. I feel as though I'm reading in a different way.

The closest village to this invisible folly, Hernhill, offers me a little of the same. Hern could come from *heron*, a link to the nearby marshes. It could also derive from the Old English for grey. Either way, the name points to this once being damp, desolate territory. But it also reminds me of Herne the Hunter, the stag-horned ghost who is thought to be an aspect of the horned god Cernunnos. This ancient deity appears in artefacts across Celtic Europe. Part human, part stag, he is associated with fertility and abundance, but also with contact with the true wild, the dark, unknowable places where death and creation are intertwined, the machinations of nature that will always be other to the human mind.

All of this is held in a name. Cernunnos takes his name from the Gaulish word *karnon*, meaning horn or antler. Karnon becomes Cernunnos. Cernunnos becomes Herne. Herne becomes a tangible presence, felt by those who spend time in the eerie solitude of the forest. You do not need to walk in the wilderness to make contact with the wild. If you know your stories – if you understand the mythologies of your land – then you can leap from a sunlit stroll with your dog into the ancient, chthonic wood.

C

In his 1973 essay 'Deep Play', the anthropologist Clifford Geertz captures the multilayered nature of profound attention. For Geertz, deep play is a game in which the players are in over their heads, usually with money at stake, but also with all the matters of status: 'esteem, honour, dignity, respect'. It is, on the face of it, a leisure activity, but one that encapsulates the whole symbolic universe of the people who partake. Deep play, in this understanding, is a macho experience – it emerges from Geertz's anthropology of cockfighting in Bali – and shows how men find ways to disrupt the hierarchies and expectations of their society, lighting a fire under the careworn everyday.

I think Geertz missed a trick. He made the boundaries of deep play too solid. I see deep play everywhere, expressed in infinite ways. It captures, for me, a quality of attention that is unexpected in adult life, and which we barely even recognise in children. That's because we misunderstand play itself, casting it as exuberant, silly, a frippery that signals to us that our children are still young enough to have not yet turned their minds to more weighty endeavours.

But play is serious. Play is absolute. Play is the complete absorption in something that doesn't matter to the external world, but which matters completely to you. It's an immersion in your own interests that becomes a feeling in itself, a potent emotion. Play is a disappearance into a space of our choosing, invisible to those outside the game. It is the pursuit of pure flow, a sandbox mind in which we can test new thoughts, new selves. It's a form of symbolic living, a way to transpose one reality onto another, and mine it for meaning. Play is a form of enchantment.

I'm always fascinated by how adults play. Conventional wisdom says that most of us lose the thread of it, our minds greying alongside our hair. But that's because we only recognise a certain kind of play, and so only associate playfulness with the adults who carry on doing the things that we expect children to do, like springing practical jokes and collecting stuffed toys. All that shows is our limited vocabulary for pleasure. It is either childlike – primary-coloured, messy, loud – or adult, dark and smoky, transgressive. These are only some of the ways it's possible to play. Deep play – those big, immersive, unprofitable processes in which we invest our whole identity – is fundamental to me, and yet mine looks dry to the outside world, colourless.

My own play has always been with words. Like many autistic children, I grew up thinking that this wasn't the right kind of play – or that it wasn't play at all in the eyes of the adults around me, who urged me to get outside, to pick up some dolls and make them fashionable, to run around a bit. I didn't want to run around. I wanted to write.

I was nine years old when I started telling people that I was planning to become a poet, but I had been writing before then. My earliest memory is sitting under the dressing table in the spare bedroom and filling pages and pages of paper with mock cursive. I didn't know the letters yet, but the impetus was there, the desire to connect things together. I remember one summer holiday when I sat at my mother's abandoned typewriter and hammered out a time-travel farce largely based on a film they'd shown at school on the last day of term. But there was a point, a distinct moment in my history, when that play hardened into something more serious. People were asking what I wanted to be when I grew up, and I wanted to be a poet.

It was cute at first. 'A poet, eh?' the adults would say, and raise their eyebrows. I knew they were laughing at me, but it was friendly enough. Everyone enjoys a little pomposity in the prepubescent. It's adorably naive, and they figure that life will knock it out of you soon enough. By the time I was thirteen, my literary ambitions elicited something closer to disgust. The sentence 'I want to be a poet' produced grunts of laughter from fellow teenagers and outright suspicion from adults. There were parodies of me all over literature, pretentious adolescents with a superior air that was not matched by talent. It was a ridiculous aspiration, and it revealed a shamefully inaccurate view of the Real World, and How It Works. 'You're a clever girl,' said my school's careers adviser. 'Have you thought of working in the prison service?'

I'd like to pretend that this was the point I decided to nurture my ambitions in secret, biding my time until I could burst forth into a kinder world, where people understood me. Instead, I stopped writing. I took all my beautiful notebooks, filled with turquoise-inked poems (okay, I regret the turquoise now), and bound them up with Sellotape, wrapping it around and around like a spider interring a fly. They were humiliating things, and I wanted to make sure nobody else could read them. I kept them on my shelf like that for a while, wondering if I'd be tempted to cut them open and take back my poems. I never did. After a while, when my connection to them felt sufficiently severed, I threw them away, burying them deep in the kitchen bin underneath the greasy butter wrappers and vegetable peelings. I can still remember the relief I felt when the dustmen came the following Monday and took them. They were irretrievably gone. I had pulled off the perfect murder.

But they haunted me like revenants. In any quiet moment, they would stand at my side and chime my own words back to me. I bitterly regretted the care with which

I'd chosen every phrase, the way that I'd finessed the metre. It made them all so painfully memorable. I was ashamed of how much they meant to me. I wished they hadn't captured so perfectly my stupid, immature, misplaced teenage emotions; I wished that I didn't still need them. I hated the idea that I'd shown them to other people, and that therefore they might still exist in the collective memory, however dilute. I thought that I might finally leave their residue when I finished school, and I took the precaution of not studying English Literature – by far my best subject – at university. Whoever I was, I had nothing to do with the act of writing. Not me.

But then, if I wasn't a writer, what was I? It felt a lot like nothing. I found myself spinning stories in my head, gathering whimsical notions and observations together, wondering how I should make my voice sound on the page. And then I would correct myself. They were old dreams, outdated habits of thought, stumbled upon by accident. If only I could find new thoughts that were just as appealing, but I couldn't. At the Freshers' Fair, I signed up for pottery class and yoga, but still I found myself straying into the offices of the student newspaper on recruitment day. Halfway through the editor's opening remarks, I thought, *God damn it, Katherine, what the hell is wrong with you? You. Are. Not. A. Writer.* I apologised and left.

I finished university and limped my way through

a series of jobs that I hated. Every single one of them seemed to spit out stories. I couldn't stop them. A daily commute to London made me yearn to write character sketches of everyone in the train carriage: the way one woman stretched her face as she applied her make-up; the man who often fell into tears of laughter over whatever was playing in his headphones. A temping job in a former mortuary made effortless ghost stories. I became obsessed with the way that one colleague, a Jehovah's Witness, tried to pass off the intrusions that the other church members made into her marriage. Having failed to conceive a child, they were concerned that she wasn't having enough sex. 'But I love my sexy times!' she exclaimed one day, her voice catching and her cheeks flushing, while we all nibbled quietly on our baguettes. It was a strain not to write it down then and there.

Writing kept coming back to me, punching its way out of whatever grave I dug it. It loomed insistent at my window. It rattled my door. I just couldn't kill it: there was no silver bullet, no stake, no incantation that would slay it. Writing had plans for me, and my resistance was futile.

I had no choice but to bargain with it. *Listen,* I said to it, *I'm going to offer you a deal. If I indulge you a little bit – take you up as a hobby, perhaps keep a diary and write the odd story to show my friends – you have to agree to settle for that. I am not willing to embarrass myself by*

trying to be a writer. I have a day job, and I don't have the
heart. I haven't read enough. I didn't study literature at
university, so I'm not entitled. But I will write in private.
And if I do that, you have to pipe down.

Writing gave no indication whether it was mollified or
not, but I carried on anyway. I went to Ikea and bought a
small table that screwed to the wall and then folded down
flat so that nobody needed to know that I'd been sitting at
it, presuming to create. On this table, I put a vase of blue
hyacinths and a fresh notebook: hardback, clothbound. I
lined up three sharp pencils. Then I pulled up a chair to
this sacrificial altar and urged myself to say something
meaningful.

After an hour, H came in to ask if I wanted anything
from the shop, and I yelled at him to get out and to leave me
alone while I was trying to write. *Trying* was the operative
word. As he closed the door, looking startled, I realised that
I had hastily shielded my notebook with both my arms,
not because it was full of my most profound thoughts, but
because it was covered in amateurish sketches of hyacinths.

Through all my brave rejection of the writing life, I
had been making one basic assumption: that writing was
my path to reject. In that hour spent in my makeshift
study, I learned many things: that a childhood talent does
not necessarily translate into an adult one; that your craft
will die if you don't nurture it; that your most profound

thoughts seem shamefully thin when they're at risk of appearing on a page. Above all, I learned what happens when you turn away from play. The most beautiful reaches of your attention degrade within you, leaving behind a residue of bitterness and frustration. In playlessness, your adult self is not nurtured, but strangled. And deep play – that play that connects across months and years, that fosters its own arcane missions, that delves into the minutiae of being – is hard to find again.

The boy who drew cats seemed unable to lose his play, even in the face of disapproving authority. He is, I think, a kind of beacon for how it ought to be done: gentle defiance. A flow towards the acts we love. We should teach this to our children. I had sailed past that point, and so I had to work to get it back. It was the labour of years, of faltering, incremental, obscure work. The skills of deep play took far longer to learn than anything I'd studied before. They meant asserting the awkward right to time, space and solitude; making a shameful claim on my own creativity. They meant learning to trust my long-forgotten gut instinct and to feel a yearning for my own work. They meant putting aside time to do things that seemed pointless to the outside world. They meant confronting my stultifying terror of failure and learning to enjoy eviscerating mediocre, mistake-ridden work. It was long and slow and uncertain, and often quite boring. I did not feel very much like the boy who drew cats, gravitating irresistibly towards my craft. I felt like someone fighting their way through undergrowth to reach a place they only vaguely remembered. That place was the core of me. Every moment was worth it.

Deep play is a labyrinth and not a maze, a twisting path with no destination. The walking is the thing. You are the walk. There is no end to it. Your only reward is more of the same – more wells to fill with your attention, more fires to tend. And every now and then, for reasons beyond your control, those fires will go out.

☾

It took H to finally find the folly. He brought his dogged, methodical mind up the hill with him, and, with map in hand, analysed all the places that a tower might be. *It can't be here, because we'd have seen it from the path. It has to be in this part of the wood.* He narrowed and narrowed his conception of where it might be. I was ready to give up. Perhaps we were on the wrong hill. Perhaps it's actually in someone's garden. I didn't have enough faith to find it myself. I didn't even believe in the map.

In the end, we didn't even need to uncover it amid a tangle of thorns. It was just there all along, exactly where it was supposed to be. Quite suddenly, we found that we could see it. We had to believe in it enough first. Its black flint walls were a perfect mimic for the dappled woodland shade, and it turned out we were looking straight at it through the leaves.

We scrambled through some bushes and over a couple of fallen trees, and there was a hexagonal tower with an open door, looking for all the world like a rook on a chess-board. Inside, it was hollow, with the evidence of a former staircase and at least one floor. No roof, no windows, and the worrying signs of masonry falling from its highest reaches. I poked my head through the door, looked up, and thought better of standing inside. But when I turned back around, Bert had become apprenticed to an old wizard who lived in the tower and was just beginning to learn that his master had a wicked streak. There was a fight between the two, the apprentice's sketchy magic nearly taking the more experienced mage by surprise. The problem was that the wizard could summon a dragon, its fiery breath surging from the windows . . .

. . . and I think about how, not so long ago, it was common to believe that dragons had actually lived in the British landscape, perhaps having only recently died out, perhaps still hidden in underground lairs. As late as the nineteenth century, there are accounts of country folk treating newts with great superstition, believing they were dragon spawn . . .

We all find our play in different places, after all. Some of us in the search for follies, some of us in the stories they suggest. What matters is that we play at all, that we nurture that particular quality of attention, that we keep up the dialogue between our play and others'. It is a flame that is worth shielding, if only because it allows us to read the contours of the land, to sense the heat pooling beneath the soil.

THE FLAMES

I'm not sure if it was the strange pattern of light coming through the windows or the general flurry of activity outside, but once again I find myself pulled out of my house, watching a fire. This time, though, I have Bert at my side, barefoot and in his pyjamas. All the neighbours are out, squinting into the dark. A column of flame is rising behind the row of houses that runs perpendicular to our street. It makes silhouettes of the rooftops and stains the sky an unnatural kind of pink. I swear I can feel its heat on my face.

We gasp. We speculate. Every one of us is clutching a phone, trying to find out more.

'Apparently it's the other side of the High Street,' says one.

'Surely it's closer than that. It looks like it's in one of those gardens. A shed?'

'A shed wouldn't burn that high. Unless it had petrol in it.'

'I assume someone's called the fire brigade.'

'I'm going to have a look.'

I stay where I am, and clutch Bert's shoulders. We are, all of us, slightly excited. Not in a ghoulish way. It is more like this fire has activated something in us that means we can't look away, that we must know everything about it, must talk over its finer points. It is an existential threat, a direct one, finally, after all the months of intangible menace. I find myself calculating how fast it could move its way towards us, at what point we would have to run. The last time I felt anything close to this was a decade ago, when I noticed that a shed was alight behind our house. While I was phoning for a fire engine the flames crossed to my own property, tearing towards me along my fence. I can still feel the heat on my face, the way that my brain knew how to calculate its speed, its progress, how much time I had to get out. I had a cat in each hand by the time the firefighters arrived. It was all quelled in a moment.

Smoke rises now, thick and black, mixing with the flames. The neighbour returns. 'Looks like it might be the school,' he says.

I feel Bert tense. I usher him inside. This is personal now, at least potentially.

'Is it my school?' he says.

'I don't know.'

'What will happen if my school burns down?'

'Let's get our facts straight first,' I say. I redouble my efforts on the phone, asking across social media and private messages, email and texts. Bert's school is positioned oddly, with no presence on any road. It is instead concealed behind terraces of houses on three sides and shops on the other. To reach it each morning, we slip down alleyways. If the school is on fire, it would explain why nobody knows what's happening. There is no direct line of sight.

'Are the teachers still in there?' asks Bert, the pitch of his voice rising.

'No,' I say. 'No. It's late. They're all home.' My phone lights up. I ignore it and try to hug him. 'It's okay. I promise it's okay.'

He shrugs me off. I read the message. It's a friend whose house backs onto the fire. She's standing in the street, she says. It's not the school. It's a disused building behind it. Everybody is safe. The fire is out.

Sometimes we are visited by destruction. Other times, it seems, the world flexes its claws and lets us feel its hot breath, just to remind us how small we are, how helpless.

I have given up on books for now – or at least, whole ones. I am trying to find the play again in my reading, in poems and articles, stories and essays. I have reset my terrifying 'to be read' pile to zero, and allowed myself the possibility of choosing new books for this age I've landed in. I have also deleted a mass of apps from my phone, and I would like to claim they were stealing my attention, but I know, really, that my attention willingly handed itself over. The ravages of this time have left me less and less keen to engage with the world in its full complexity. I have been shying away from thought itself. I have wanted to be distracted.

A change is coming, whether or not I am paying attention. Life is no longer the same. I can feel it in the people around me: the scramble to get away from it, the terror that it might touch us, the urge to stay high and dry. I can feel us calcifying, separating, drawing in. I hope the change brings justice for the people who deserve it, not punishment for those who don't. I hope we can all rise above the urge for petty revenge. I hope the change brings justice rather than suffering, connection rather than more rancour. I hope, most of all, that we can learn to soften into this time and into each other. To merge again, somehow. To melt back into the landscapes that hold us, and that are still releasing the wisdom of millennia, quietly, slowly, if only we can learn to listen.

Change is the restless bedrock on which we're founded. Lauren Olamina, the heroine of Octavia E. Butler's Earthseed series, makes a god out of change itself, 'the only lasting truth in the world'. For her, the sacred is found in adaptation. Perhaps this is what I'm seeking too, the ability to step into the world's flux, to travel with it rather than rasping against it, to let my own form dance across it. 'We do not worship God,' Lauren writes in verse. 'We perceive and attend to God / We learn from God . . . We shape God.' It's as good a truth as any, as holy a space in which to rest our minds: we are not the passive recipients of the numinous, but the active constructors of a pantheon. We make the change, and it makes us. Entering into that exchange – knowing the depths of permanence and the restlessness of movement – is the work of a lifetime.

How do we meet this kind of god, this irresistible force that roars through our existence like a hurricane? We adapt. We evolve. We rebuild and remake and renew. We listen to what it has to tell us, and undertake the work of integrating the new knowledge. Sometimes we read it in books. Sometimes we read it elsewhere, in scents carried on the air and the flight paths of birds. Sometimes we need to feel the tingle of magic to remind us what we believe.

☾

My cheap fire bowl is wearing thin now, because I keep on using it whenever I need to mark something, whenever I need to make something feel real. Tonight, standing in my garden on a damp September evening, I am trying to reintegrate fire back into our own mythology, to make it safe again. Fire is only as safe as our behaviour around it, I always tell Bert. We bring this unruly force into our lives to remind ourselves of what enchantment means: a practice at the edges of the power that sears through all existence. It will never, ever be ours to control. It will always demand our respect, our careful conduct, our close attention.

We have been to visit the burned-out building today, to peer at it through the police tape and take in its desolation. Bert needed to see it. In his mind, it was still burning and would burn on forever, a perpetual threat. In reality, it is cold and damp, the skeleton of a building that we never knew whole. There are twists of metal, and wood charred so black that it's velvety, like animal pelt. It is, in its own way, tamed.

I throw a sheaf of bay tree prunings onto my fire, the leaves dry and bronze. They crackle, and I breathe in the scented smoke. A flare of flame, and then I watch the heat surge red through the narrow twigs, making them capillaries. Then they're gone, burned through, and the fire is working its way more slowly along the fatter branches, patterning them with its hunger. It is like witnessing desire in action, the way the fire lusts for its fuel. Whatever happens – whatever I do – all this will be ash in the morning. It is not my business to stand in the way of fire. I am ready, I think, to submit to it now, this new world and the new ways I must live in it. It has just taken me a while to see it, to accept it as part of my lot.

After the night the stars fell in 1833, its witnesses rushed to understand. Scientists compared measurements and wrote papers, and looked back in history to notice patterns that had been there all along, but which had been scarcely recognised. In mid-November every thirty-three years, give or take some dating errors and some minor variations in the path of the comet Tempel–Tuttle, somewhere in the world experiences a spectacular meteor shower as the earth passes through its debris. The true wonder surely lies in how often we've forgotten it.

But science was not the only way that people came to understand the starfall and to draw out its meanings. 'The people were frightened and thought that the end had come,' wrote Harriet Powers, the folk artist who depicted the meteor shower on a quilt that now forms part of the Smithsonian's collection. 'God's hand staid the stars.' The starfall took place long before Powers was born into slavery in 1837, but by the time she was old enough to stitch quilts, it had become a landmark in time for African Americans who had been denied access to their own dates of birth, their own parentage. The night the stars fell became a fixed point by which speakers could navigate as they came to tell their own stories, and oral histories of the time allowed future generations to piece back together fractured histories. The writer and genealogist Angela Y. Walton-Raji was able to estimate the birthdate of her great-great-grandmother Amanda from her account of that night, 'which she spoke of, over and over till her death, in 1920'. People who witnessed the starfall could do nothing but speak of it, and their voices reverberated into the future.

The starfall echoed through all our ways of knowing. It appeared in song lyrics and book titles: it was referenced in literary works from William Faulkner to N. Scott Momaday. Abraham Lincoln was fond of drawing on the Leonids as a metaphor for how the Union would endure – the fixed stars remained in their place despite the war that raged over their surface. The spectacle did not have one consistent effect, nor did it lead to any fixed conclusions, but instead it sparked fascination, engagement, and leaps in comprehension, forcing people to reach for new modes of expression and fresh understandings. It united people in their common attention and scattered disparate meanings across the firmament. When we look for enchantment to give us direct, concrete revelations, we miss the point. It is too big for us to swallow all at once. It teaches us in constellations, and invites us to undertake the slow lifelong work of assimilating a moment.

AIR

IN FLIGHT

We have just made it into the air when someone peels an orange, and the whole plane fills with the scent of quiet afternoons with my grandmother.

I know this trick: it is a ward against travel sickness. I have always been unsettled in motion. I like my feet on solid ground. I have queasily peeled oranges on coaches, cross-channel ferries, and in the back seats of cars. I sometimes catch their potency in a paper bag to concentrate the effect. An orange cuts through nausea like a scalpel, even if the effect is only temporary.

Maybe this person is just like me, anonymous in a sea of identical chair backs. Maybe they, too, feel the dislocation of flight. I do not trust planes. I can never quite grasp their mechanics, the way that they can be held by nothing but air. They are, for me, an act of faith, but in science rather than in God. I have to trust that my own understanding is inadequate and that others know better than me. Next to me, Bert grips my hand in a way that suggests he feels the same. We have both been chewing gum to release the pressure in our ears. I offer him a tissue to

spit the gum into and then a bottle of water. The air hisses
free as I unscrew the lid. This possibly explains why I am
dizzy again.

I can always meditate on trains, but never in planes.
It is not a simple matter of movement. It is instead about
contact. Mid-air, my attention has nowhere to sink – just
an unsteady void below, seven miles of nothing. Up here, I
cannot put down roots. I am in transit, in a state between
two solidities. Flying feels like an intermission in the real
business of living.

We are returning from a necessary journey. We have
visited my mother in Spain for the first time since the
pandemic separated us. Bert swam in the multitude of
outdoor pools that dot the landscape (you can see them
from above as you land, blue unblinking eyes gazing up
at you). I made sure that everything was okay. I wanted to
cross one more thing off my list of vigilances. Up here in
the air, I hope this knowledge will add a little ballast to my
free-floating attention. Perhaps it will anchor me again.

The plane lurches, and Bert says, 'What was that?'

'Turbulence,' I say. 'Nothing to worry about.'

I remember how I learned to trust those sudden drops
in altitude by measuring what is spilled. The water barely judders in my bottle. The flight attendants continue
on their way up their aisle without a flinch. In the vast
reaches of the open skies, these jolts that trouble us so

much are nothing at all, an infinitesimally small descent in relation to where we have climbed. But the human body is mistrustful of falls, and so we brace all the same.

The problem is that air is strange to us. We do not understand its formlessness, its transparency. Its meanings pass too easily through our fingers.

There is one thing I want to do as soon as I get home again. I drive down to the southernmost tip of my county and park in a residential street near Greatstone Beach, the same place I used to visit as a child. But today I am not interested in the dunes or the sea (I'd only have to hoover the car). Instead, I walk in the opposite direction, down the side of the Romney Sands Holiday Park and onto the fields of gravel.

Sometimes, for a special treat, I used to take the little train along here with my grandad when everyone else was at the beach. My mother would drop us off along the route, and we would board the Romney, Hythe & Dymchurch Railway, a collection of tiny trains that have trundled on tracks only fifteen inches apart since the 1920s. Most of the rolling stock still runs on steam. Travelling on this line means crouching into a tiny carriage, rolling past the myriad sheep of Romney Marsh and then along the backs of houses until you reach the bleak, beloved wasteland of Dungeness, with its strange quality of light and looming power station. I loved it then because I adored being escorted anywhere by my grandad, who always banged his head on the way in and out, and couldn't resist stopping for a chat with the engine driver. I love it now because the smell of coal and steam, and the shine of the well-tended engines, bring me back to the perfect contentment of those moments.

I hear the train as I'm striking out from the rows of caravans – its owly shriek that echoes across the flat ground. It trundles past, puffing out steam, and I think perhaps I catch the scent of it. I am on a path now between two deep, tantalising lakes that rustle with reeds. And then they appear: the concrete ears of Dungeness. They stand proudly behind the lakes, their grey bowls tilted optimistically towards the sky.

These acoustic mirrors were positioned all over the Kent coast in the late 1920s, offering an early warning system for incoming planes. The two huge dishes at Dungeness – twenty and thirty feet respectively – could catch and concentrate the sound waves emitted by incoming aircraft, which were then relayed back through a microphone to an operator. A third sound mirror, a two-hundred-foot curved wall, was built shortly after. With a range of around twenty-four miles on a clear day, at best they gave a fifteen-minute warning of any invasion, less still as aircraft grew faster. Nearly as soon as they were installed, they were superseded by radar, which actively projected out radio waves instead of passively waiting for sound to arrive.

They stand now as relics, a discarded technology, really known only by word of mouth. But to me, they hold their own enchantment. When I studied physics as a teenager, I struggled to believe in the sound waves that I copied into my folder in diagrammatic form. I didn't truly accept that they existed until I saw the listening ears and learned how they caught these undulating pathways of sound and made them bounce into a focal point, where they could be harvested and heard. The sound mirrors externalise an invisible process and show us the narrow range of our own perception. There is so much, always, that we don't see. There is so much that we don't hear. The air is full of information. We just have to find the right way to listen.

The Dungeness ears are one of my sacred places, a subject of my repeated pilgrimage. It seems that they gather more than sound waves. They condense, for me, a tangle of difficult feelings – of nostalgia, grief, outsidership – and render them back into air again. I can visit them and be quiet for a while, loving the smooth brutality of their concrete, the way they merge into a landscape that can only ever be an edgeland anyway. It feels as though otherness clusters on Dungeness: nuclear reactors, trains of uncanny size, houses made of nothing but scrap. And me, of course, bringing my unsettled feelings to a place where they feel at home.

A little further along the peninsula is Prospect Cottage, the black tarred shack where Derek Jarman retreated in his final years. Dying of AIDS, the director transformed the house into a text, covering the walls in books and paintings and poetry. John Donne's poem 'The Sunne Rising' is inscribed on an outside wall, hand-cut from marine plywood in Jarman's own handwriting. 'Busy old fool, unruly sun / Why dost thou thus, / Through windows, and through curtains call on us?' Peter Fillingham, the artist who installed it, says that Jarman dreamed up each new improvement to the cottage during his long stays in hospital, and would call up his friends to share his plans. In this way, life was infused into the fabric of the building, even as its owner faded out. 'Love, all alike, no season knows nor clime,' reads the poem. 'Nor hours, days, months, which are the rags of time.'

Best known is the garden that Jarman raised from the shingle around Prospect Cottage, sparsely decorated with the few plants that could survive the perpetual Dungeness winds, and with driftwood and rusted metal that washed up on the nearby beach. 'People thought I was building a garden for magical purposes,' he wrote. 'I saw it as a therapy.' But surely he could not deny that his garden came to feel like an act of witchcraft, to raise an oasis in such thin soil, to enchant a place to the extent that he did. When I visited Prospect Cottage on a rare open day, not long after his death, the little house seeped peace from its very walls. That is no mean feat of transfiguration.

Lost souls have long retreated to the seaside to take the air. But only here, where concrete ears manifest the invisible, does the purpose become clear. The air is a place of letting go. Its business is dispersal, the dissipation of fog, the scattering of seeds. Subtly, imperceptibly, air brings in the new.

GLORIES

In the last years of the eighteenth century, a young man called J. Lud. Jordan decided to ascend the Brocken, the highest mountain in northern Germany. The Harz mountain range could be a forbidding place, rife with legends of witches and demons, but on this day in late May it was beautiful. Setting out before dawn, he watched the sky redden, and then the sun seemed to burst from the horizon, rendering the landscape – and the walker – serene. A mist began to gather around the mountains below him, soon becoming a thick fog.

He climbed the *Teufelskanzel*, the Devil's Pulpit, an outcrop of granite that Goethe had used as the setting for a satanic orgy in *Faust*. Standing at the top, he looked over towards the peak of the Wormberg and saw something that stopped his breath: a figure of a giant man standing as if on a pedestal. It was a fleeting vision. Even as Jordan watched, the mists thinned below him and the apparition vanished.

Jordan's was a small encounter, and in many ways unremarkable amid all the strange tales told by those who have ventured into our most extreme places. Sublime landscapes are liminal spaces that divorce us from the comfortable everyday and take us to the edge of understanding. As we cling to the living side of that edge, we often glimpse something of the other side. Despite this, Jordan doesn't overstate his case. His observations are more about the splendour of the wild than the menace of the occult. He published a short account in the *Göttingen Journal of Natural Science* and it was copied faithfully in its original German into the notebook of Samuel Taylor Coleridge, who, thirty years later, used the image in a poem. In this account, the spirit becomes an image of naive self-deception. It is worshipped by a woodman, who does not realise it is his own shadow.

And that is exactly what a Brocken spectre is: a person's shadow cast onto cloud cover by a low-lying sun, stretched out into eerie proportions by the angle of projection. This effect is heightened by the fact that the shadow is often disconnected from the viewing subject's feet, breaking our familiarity with the form. The shifting nature of the clouds and mists onto which they are projected means that the spectres can appear to move in curious ways, and we find it hard to judge how far away the shadow actually is, meaning that we can vastly overestimate its size. What is missing from Jordan's account (although it's crucial to Coleridge's poem) is the most interesting feature of the phenomenon, the factor that elevates the sighting from curious to uncanny: the presence of the 'glory', a shimmering rainbow halo around the giant's head. Brocken spectres often seem to inspire feelings of terror or doom in those who encounter them. Although it's hard to find an account in which the viewer doesn't eventually realise that the strange creature is mirroring their movements, they are sometimes suggested as a worldly explanation for angelic sightings.

The glory itself is the effect of light refracting through water droplets in a similar way to a rainbow. It is centred on the antisolar point, the place directly opposite the sun according to the viewer, which is, of course, the viewer's head. This is why the glory appears as a halo: it is positioned by our gaze, rather than existing independently in the space above the clouds. When groups of people encounter the right conditions, they see groups of spectres, but each viewer will only see one glory, centred on their own shadow.

I have always dreamed of seeing a Brocken spectre for myself. My Usborne *The World of the Unknown: Ghosts*, which I studied intensively as a child, showed the Brocken spectre as an ethereal creature stretched across the landscape, and as was true of most of the case studies in that book, I both dreaded ever happening across such a thing and also hoped ardently that I would. As I got older, I understood the science, but the first-hand accounts I read still suggested that the appearance of the spectre would confound my analytical brain and make me believe that the mountains were patrolled by ethereal beings. By the time I finally saw a photograph of a Brocken spectre, I was already disenchanted. The advent of the internet brought pictures taken by hikers, usually blurry affairs captured on mobile phones and early digital cameras. They were compelling, certainly, but they were also nothing at all, a triangulated shadow with prismatic hair. I found it hard to imagine being confronted by that in real life and believing in its supernatural force for anything more than a couple of seconds.

In *Memories, Dreams, Reflections*, Carl Jung notes a dream he had when he was eighteen, in which he was carrying a tiny light through a foggy landscape when he felt a presence behind him and turned to see a 'gigantic black figure' following him. On waking, he realised immediately that it had been a Brocken spectre, 'my own shadow on the swirling mists'. The Brocken spectre is a ghost of our own making, a literal projection of the dark part of our self onto an unstable surface. When we raise a hand, it raises a hand in response, except that it looks as though it might almost touch the arc of the sky. When we run, it runs, except that it strides over mountains where we stumble over rocks. It is us made

significant, a glory poised around its head as if it might
know the answers to the mysteries of the universe. It is
us passed to the other side, bearing the angelic corona
that marks out the dead and the forgiven. It is our shadow self, writ large across the clouds. When we stumble
upon an encounter with these things, why would we not
drink in their potency for a few seconds before we reason
them away?

We can know exactly how these phenomena operate
and still be swept away by their *unheimlich* qualities.
We can suspend disbelief and use these experiences as
gateways into a different kind of consciousness. We can
hold both within us and feel no friction between them.
We have Western accounts of Brocken spectres dating
back nearly three hundred years (and far more ancient
ones from Buddhist monasteries), and in nearly every
single one of them, the witness comes to ask how, in the
material world, this effect was created. Our ancestors
had a more agile way of travelling through the world,
dancing between what they could observe and what
they could construct, spinning out meanings as they
passed through the wild. We think we've advanced
since then, but instead we've jettisoned our capacity
to accommodate the complex interplay of symbolic and
rational thought, the scientific and the enchanted. Both
have their own mode of wonder, their own sublimities,

their own awes. Where a seething ecosystem once flour-ished, there is now the silence of the explained world.

I hope that perhaps one day I will see my own Brocken spectre. I think it will most likely happen on a clifftop with an early morning sun at my back. It would have to be the right clifftop at the right time and in the right sea-son, but mountains have never been my domain. When I say I have no head for heights, I mean it quite literally: the fragile balance of fluid in my ears is entirely toppled at altitude. I had to be nearly carried down from that first mountain I climbed as a Girl Guide, my vision spinning.

But during one of my routine searches for new sight-ings, I learned that there is a place in Yorkshire that has gained a reputation for Brocken spectres. On the boundary between Burley Moor and Ilkley Moor, there is apparent-ly the perfect spot: a fog gathers on cold mornings, and a low sun can send your silhouette slanting across it. I have little hope that I could contrive to actually see my own spectre in this way – after all, it's a six-hour drive away, and the exact weather conditions are nearly impossible to predict. But I want to go there anyway. I want to be in the place where the spectres have been.

My friend Kate agrees to meet me for an early walk, rising from the village of Burley Woodhead and up onto the moors. Kate is a Yorkshire native whose own writing has often explored the meaning of being a northerner. I am just an enthusiastic visitor, but a repeat one. I adore Yorkshire. We used to stay in the Dales every New Year, just for the chance to see snow amid the grand scenery. I don't think Yorkshire's claim to be 'God's own country' is far off. It's certainly big enough, and its beauty is austere and serious, as befits a being with all of creation on their mind.

Today the moor is covered in muted purple heather, and the sky is thunderous. As we make our way from the road onto the Dales Way, I remember the pleasure of having a map in my hand. We try to assess how long it has been since we last saw each other. We think perhaps three years. Everything has changed since then, but nothing has changed between us. I find it easy to tell Kate that I haven't been able to read, despite the fact that she reads everything. I know that she will, at least, understand the loss.

As we continue up the steep track, I realise that Kate is wheezing. Asthma, she says. It has made an unwelcome return since she had Covid. There is not enough air for her today. We slow our pace, and her breathing slows, too. I am not the only one adapting to an aftermath in which I'm changed. Mine is a small loss, really, and certainly recoverable. We finally break onto high, flat ground, where it feels as though the whole world is laid out before us. The moors bristle with rugged life. To the north-east, the clouds have broken and there is light spill over a distant town.

Ahead of us is an outcrop of grey sandstone known as the Cow and Calf, the landmark we've chosen to aim for. We cross a stream and I filter us both some water so that we can imbibe this place. The water is soft and delicate, and unspeakably welcome to a dry mouth unused to hills. I try to explain the potency I feel when I drink the water in the midst of a walk, the way that I feel I've integrated myself into the landscape a little more. Aloud, and here in the practical North, I'm worried that it sounds a little like I've been spending too much time alone. But it doesn't matter. We are deep into the kind of fluid, winding chatter that draws together all of heaven and earth anyway. We are up high together, with aching legs, and our stories billow around each other, their particles merging. Everything is permissible. Everything is understood.

I wonder how the spectres could possibly appear here until I see it, an abrupt falling away of the land towards the west, creating a bowl beneath us. Today it is filled with the same bracken and heather as the rest of the moor, but I can imagine the mist gathering here on cold, bright mornings, when everything is quiet and still, starkly gothic in the way that only Yorkshire can be. Then you could believe that your own shadow was anything, stealing away across the wilderness. I am certain that it could speak to something atavistic in me.

We climb up to the Cow and Calf and sit down to drink tea from our flasks, gazing over the town. Up close, the rocks are alive in a way that I hadn't expected: they are covered in names and dates, chiselled into the soft sandstone by extremely well-equipped walkers. Most of the graffiti is Victorian and impressively neat. Robinsons and MacDonalds, Marshalls and Bramleys, Ogdens and Lovells are all memorialised in perfect copperplate, although one repeat offender reverses all his capital Ns. These people climbed up here a hundred and fifty years ago and applied themselves to creating a kind of eternity for their names. I later learn that there are Bronze Age carvings here, too, hidden amongst the more recent noise. I wish that I had searched for them instead of for my own ghost.

But for now I tell Kate that we used to sing about this place in school music lessons when the teacher wanted an easy hour: 'On Ilkla Moor *Baht'at*', a song in Yorkshire dialect, in which a young man is scolded for going courting on the moor *baht'at* – without a hat on. He is told he will catch his death of cold, which leads to some fairly gruesome consequences: the worms will eat him, and then the ducks will eat the worms. Eventually his friends will eat the ducks, which means, as the speaker triumphantly proclaims, '*Then us will all have eaten thee . . . That's where we get our own back.*' It is not quite clear why such an act of revenge needs to be taken for a minor sin of omission. Surely we have all forgotten to wrap up warmly enough in moments of youthful enthusiasm? But that is perhaps not the point. All of life and death is on Ilkley Moor, and those of us who pass through it – whether we eat its ducks or drink its water – cannot but help be part of its cycle. It's no wonder our ancestors felt the need to carve their names onto rocks.

Driving south again through the proud Yorkshire landscape, I feel as though I am a little rebalanced. I have been living an awful lot inside my own head, foggy though it has been. Perhaps, in retrospect, the fog was necessary. After all, if beings as marvellous as Brocken spectres can be projected onto fog, then perhaps it can also serve as a screen onto which I can cast the flickering new self that I have been imagining.

I have found something to set free in all this billowing air. It is a small, cramped shadow hiding in me, which tells me that I am stupid to see magic everywhere, that I am embarrassing myself. But Brocken spectres show me how to tread the horizon between blunt rationality and the spiralling interpretations that might lift it into greater meaning. Certainly we do not have to enchant these shadows. We could choose to leave them merely explained. But it now seems to me that we humans have capacity for more: for another layer of experience, for an extra depth of understanding. I no longer understand why we would not reach for this.

KEEPING

It is early spring, I'm back to the classroom, but this time without the folders and books, the rulers and highlighter pens. I am trying to learn through my hands. This is not how I was trained, and I am twitchy with the need to inscribe a margin down the side of clean white paper, and to transform the words coming out of the lecturer's mouth into my untidy handwriting, preferably verbatim. But no, that is not what I'm doing today.

I have fallen foul of this urge before. My first week of university, I attended an introductory lecture from a very famous sociologist. I think we were supposed to be awed by his presence, but that was impossible if you didn't know who he was in the first place.

'Don't take notes,' he said. 'I just want you to listen.'

I took notes. I didn't trust listening. It was prone to decomposition over time. I wanted to make sure I would capture this new knowledge, so I opened my notepad and started to write. It was unfortunate that I was sitting in the front row, but all the other seats were taken by the time I'd arrived, flustered by my inability to follow a map.

He was waving two recent newspapers in the air and telling us that they represented the key concerns of sociology – what they were I now don't remember – and was pacing around like a matador in a stadium. For a moment, he broke away from this polished piece of theatre to say, 'As I said, no need to take notes.' A smirk. 'You will not be examined on this.'

It was spoken to the crowd, and everyone laughed. I dropped my pen for a while and tried to listen, but I found that I couldn't do it. Sitting still and absorbing information seemed like two opposing forces to me. I needed to do something active to stop my mind from focusing on my body rather than on what was being said. I needed to write it down, or else to get up and pace the room. I felt certain that he would not have liked the latter option, and besides, he was now talking about essay titles and how work should be submitted, and was taking us through a reading list which he said should by now have been provided to us by our colleges. Mine had not arrived.

Panicked, I started to take notes again, trying to capture every title, every partially heard name which I hoped, with a little ingenuity, I could find in the library index cards later. I had become quite absorbed in the urgency of this task, when I felt the unmistakable quickening of the air that comes when someone is rushing towards you, and a hand thudded flat across my page, knocking my pen sideways.

'I said *don't write anything down*,' said the lecturer. The humour was gone from his voice now, but that didn't stop the whole room from laughing.

I probably didn't take the lesson from this he wanted me to. I didn't think: *Oh, I must ease up on the compulsion to trap every new piece of information onto the page.* Instead, I doubled down. Writing, for me, is a way of making the airy matter of thought feel real. I can open up a notebook and solidify my feelings, which otherwise seem to float around my head, ill-defined, mutable. It is a necessary act of anchoring. I am not remotely sorry that I attempted to tether myself to the unknown language of my new degree by writing it all down, and I have rarely been sorry since. The only thing that troubles me in general is finding the thoughts I've so carefully stored amid all those reams of paper. I also fear that the ceiling will one day fall through under the weight of all the notebooks stored in the attic.

But here, today, I appear to have forgotten my notebook, and so I am cast out into the open waters without my familiar life raft. The tutor is unpacking his equipment and talking us through how it is used, the different forms it can take. 'I'm glad to see no one is taking notes,' he says. 'Today's all about the experience.' Distrustful of my own memory, I take photos instead, the same as I do on walks. I can go back through them later and probably make notes.

He glances out of the window and says, 'The rain's cleared up. Let's go and see the bees.'

The bees are what I'm here for: the promise of unpacking a hive and seeing first-hand the industry of making honey. I have long dreamed of hosting a colony in my own garden, not for any particular love of the sweet stuff, but just to know the bees themselves, to understand their arcane knowledge of the air. I think perhaps it might be impossible in my small garden. The bees won't mind, but my neighbours might. I am not convinced that other people like bees as much as I do. I have, after all, spent the last few weeks being asked, 'Don't you mind getting stung?'

But in any case, I have learned today that it is possible to keep bees in a small urban garden like mine, as long as you enclose them in a six-foot fence. This forces them to fly upward before they strike off across the patchwork of gardens in search of flowers, creating a flight path that stays above most people's heads. My alternative plan is to install them on the roof of the garden office that I always dream of building. Either way, I will need to be decisive. Once you have set up your hive, we are told, you can move it three inches or three miles, but nothing in between. A honeybee's navigation is so precise that it will not be able to find a hive that has been moved to the other side of the garden lawn.

I step into the voluminous white beekeeper's boiler suit with its tightly elasticated sleeves. I fold the legs carefully into my wellington boots. I have to be airtight – or at least bee-tight – to ensure that no furious hymenopteran finds its way into my only line of defence. A hood zips on top. We are warned not to let the mesh touch our faces, because the bees can sting through it. Not, says our tutor, that the bees we'll meet today are aggressive. But sometimes . . . every now and then . . . We are advised, when the time comes, to buy well-tempered bees – probably the Buckfast variety, renowned for their good nature – and to keep a careful eye on their behaviour in case they breed with undesirables from another colony. Finally we put on our kid gloves and walk out across damp fields.

Three National Beehives stand by a hedgerow, with very few bees in sight. It is beginning to drizzle, and bees hate rain. They have all drawn inwards. Before we can meet them, we must prepare our smoker. We are shown how to light dried grass in the bottom of a stainless-steel flask with a conical top. The wafts of smoke subdue the bees by blocking their ability to detect the pheromone signals that would otherwise alert them to an intruder. It makes them forget to attack, and instead they dive down into the hive to tend to their honey. Our tutor lifts off the first layer of the hive, and there they are: the wooden frames of honeycomb, crowded by bees.

He puffs on some smoke, and the brazen ones that had already risen up to confront us sink placidly down again. A high whine rises, the sound of fifty thousand fairly contented bees.

'Listen carefully as I do this,' he says, and takes a hive tool out of his pocket, something between a hook and a crowbar that neatly levers out the hanging frames. The note of the hive rises, a definite ratcheting up of hostilities.

'They're fine,' he says. Another puff of smoke.

One by one, we are allowed to approach the hive to handle the bees. I watch the people before me, my hands aching to do their own learning. When my time comes, I approach the hive and feel the heat it exudes. Clumsily I hook the tool under a frame and ease out one corner, feeling its sticky crack. It is not honey that has glued it in place, but propolis, the substance that bees make from tree resin, which they use to hold their hive together, waterproof it, and protect it from bacteria and spores. It carries a whiff of antiseptic, a woody assurance of safety. I inch the tool into the other side, and the note of the colony rises once again. They are so loud when they all sing together, and with the smell of honey and propolis, the smoke, the way the whole box vibrates under your hands, it is quite absolute, this interaction of human and bee. I feel as though we are able to speak to each other, however imperfectly.

I know that I will transmit something if I deal with them calmly and firmly. They need the reassurance of steady hands. So I lift out the frame as though I know exactly what I am doing, and feel the shocking weight of them, these creatures that are light enough to overcome the air, but which also mass together in numbers that make them heavy. Their amber bodies bustle against one another as they work over their hexagonal cells. I am shown the capped honey that is being stored for winter; the uncapped nectar that will still be too watery for honey; the bulging yellow cells in which drones and workers are pupating. Later another student will lift out a frame from which a worker is emerging, eating its way through the waxy cap. But here, on my frame, everything is calm. I turn it over – that weight, again, against my fingers makes me afraid that I will drop it – and inspect the other side.

The bees are growing discontented now, pinging upwards as though held on hidden wires. Time to put them back again. Carefully, carefully, I slot the frame back in and step back, exhilarated. I have learned a lot about bees today, and only some of it is factual. Most of it is muscle memory. Most of it is understood in the pitch and intensity of a note that I could not find on a stave. Most of it is reciprocal, an intent, speechless duty of care.

In *Braiding Sweetgrass*, the Native American botanist Robin Wall Kimmerer makes a powerful case for a return to the indigenous understanding of the land, based on careful stewardship, deep knowledge and reciprocity. When we know the detail of the places we inhabit – when we tend them with our own hands and walk them with our own feet – we enter into a conversation with our places that is mutually nourishing. We learn to listen to the ways in which they speak to us, and to find a way to reply so that they can understand. This congress is a series of gifts shared, rather than any kind of simple transaction. Behind it all is a sense of enchantment, a belief that sentience flows through all the inhabitants of the natural world, both animate and inanimate, and a calling to enter a continuous state of wonder at its functioning and flow.

One way to work towards this stewardship is to be skilled within our own landscape, to foster ways of tending to its needs as we meet our own. We are, I think, only too painfully aware of these lost skills. Native Americans are still living a history that saw these practices forcibly taken from them. My own community lost them through indifference. The small, precise gestures that make up a skill set seemed so ordinary until we let them slip away. But now that they are gone, they are very hard to reclaim. They are part of a web of intuitions and abilities so fundamentally interconnected that relearning them will be a life's work. They range from being able to hold a paring knife correctly to learning to read the weather. From understanding properties of different types of wood to knowing how to preserve food.

This is not just a matter of knowledge, but also a matter of desire. We have forgotten how to want one good dress over fifty disposable ones. We have forgotten how to crave each new food as it comes into season. We must learn to know with our hands rather than our heads.

I often think that growing up in my grandparents' house, where we still seemed to be living out an approximation of the 1940s, was a stroke of luck. I absorbed a yearning for the many different forms of peace that dwelt in that house, and a taste for the things that it held in reverence. Time moved more slowly there. The afternoons were long. Everything we owned was carefully kept and mended. Even to people of my own age, I find it hard to describe the excitement that we shared at every new vegetable that my grandad brought in from the garden. I am still inexplicably moved at the sight of a freshly cut January King cabbage, its engorged leaves, the way it holds drops of water like jewels.

I do not live the restricted life that my grandparents lived. I do not enjoy the monotony quite so much. But I've carried a few residual skills with me, which I find myself leaning towards as I get older. If I find a hole in my sweater, I can graft it back together so that the repair is invisible. I can sew on a button so that it stays attached. I can identify a field mushroom and make a cake without a recipe. I can tell a damson from a sloe, a cobnut from a hazelnut; can work out exactly the right time to pick a blackberry. They are small skills, but they are mine, and I'm determined to pass them on. The greatest part of them is not the skill itself but the culture that surrounds it. Those blackberries and damsons like to be asked first before they're pulled from their branch. That's how you'll know when they're ripe. You take only what you need, transform it into something good, and give away a portion of what you've made. You have, after all, received it as a gift. It would be selfish not to pass it on.

Explaining these things out loud makes me feel like an anthropologist describing some distant culture that has been hidden away from Western eyes for all of history. But that's because these laws for living were never meant to be articulated in that way. They were supposed to be absorbed through observation and practice, and never subjected to something so clumsy as the page. This is how most people learned for most of history. It's another skill we could reclaim.

When the Micronesian master navigator Mau Piailug died in 2010, he took some of that knowledge with him. Mau had learned to sail by the stars, the wind, and the behaviour of the sea; he spoke of the talk of the water and the talk of the light. Taught by his grandfather from infanthood, Mau memorised his map of the heavens from a star compass made of beach pebbles laid out on the shore. It was never allowed to be written down. It was the work of years, more agile than anything set in text. He knew over one hundred stars in this way, where they rose and set, where they might lead. In 1976 he used this knowledge to navigate alone from Hawaii to Tahiti, a voyage of 2,500 miles that archaeologists speculated had once been undertaken by ancient seafarers. Mau proved that it was possible, and in the process sparked a move-ment to preserve his extraordinary knowing. Except that Mau acknowledged that his pupils would need a key con-cession if this knowledge was to survive: they would have to write everything down.

I'm not suggesting that we should unlearn this mod-ern age entirely and revert back to some fantasised simpler time. There was never a moment when we had it right, and this era we live in now is full of miraculous ways to come together and to adapt. But it is time for a reckoning. We have run as far as we can from the hardships of previous ages, and now we need to find a balance between what we know and what we knew. If we start to re-enchant the most fundamental parts of our existence – the food, the objects that we use, the places we inhabit – we can begin to restore our connection between our bodies and the land. This can't be achieved in the abstract. We must learn to become better keepers of the things that matter.

I am in a bee suit and boots again, trying not to let the veil touch my face. The same smell of smoke and propolis, the same industrious hum. I wait impatiently to be invited to lift out a frame and inspect the bees and their comb, to assess the quantity of honey and the composition of the brood cells. I am perhaps a little more eager than the other learners, a little less anxious about what the bees might do. I have already learned to trust them. I just don't quite trust myself yet.

When I booked my beekeeping course, I thought that I would go home ready to keep my own bees. I thought that I would order myself a hive, a bee suit and a box of bees (they come by post, weighed by the kilo), and set off on my own to make honey. I could still, technically, do that, but I realise now that this was never what I really wanted. There is a craft here, a labyrinthine system of knowledge that is best learned from others. I want to take it slowly, to absorb my lessons through the skin and the ears, to sometimes get stung. I'm determined to know it deeply before I go any further, and there are plenty of people who are willing to teach me. It seems to me there is a different kind of congregation out there, sharing a different kind of worship. I want to connect with them, rather than to fly off on my own.

The keeper I'm learning from today gives us latex gloves instead of kid gauntlets – the better, he says, to meet the bees. Without anything at all, the colony would swarm over your hands for the scents that linger on them. But the thin gloves offer all the protection you need. These are trustworthy bees, and they do not want to sting you. Handle them respectfully, and they'll know you're not a threat. I'm already coming to understand that each keeper is different in philosophy and approach, and that there is no one way of doing things. It's interesting to observe and absorb, and to wonder what kind of keeper I'll be when I'm better at this. Today's style is lower on smoke and therefore higher on bees buzzing around your ears and crawling over your sleeves. We are, all of us, dotted with them. They pattern our suits as they explore us, inch by inch, as if we might just be a peculiar kind of flower they have yet to meet.

'Here,' he says, 'you can touch them. Be gentle. They won't sting.' He holds out a frame of crawling amber bodies, all busying over their cells. I reach out my hand and hover it above them, feeling their vibration rise to meet me. Then slowly, carefully, I rest the backs of my fingers onto the bees, and I feel their heat, their life, their motion. Then they disperse, and I am touching the honey they have set in their comb, ready for winter.

'Taste it,' he says, and I do, awkwardly unzipping my hood to reach my mouth. It is floral, sweet and slightly lemony, pleasingly bitter, more complex by far than anything on a supermarket shelf. Different, too, from the local honey that's sold in jars at the greengrocer. Here, in this moment, an understanding is captured: of the world as it tastes to a bee, of flavours so ephemeral that they can't be bottled, of what it is to share a knowing with your colony.

THE SEED OF ALL THAT EXISTS

For my last birthday, somebody gave me a packet of wildflower seeds tucked inside a card. I am not much of a gardener. I don't have a neat potting shed with trays of saved seeds. I left the packet on the kitchen worktop, and when, after a week, a cup of tea got spilled on it, I nearly threw it out. But I reasoned that there was no harm in scattering them across the garden – there was a small chance of flowers this way, and zero chance if I put them in the bin. So I cast them out across the soil and hoped the rain would take them into the soil.

As I've got older, I've noticed that all my friends have gradually become excellent custodians of their gardens, but I have not. I'm more than a little embarrassed by this. It feels like the kind of thing I should do, but growing just doesn't seem to happen for me. I like to blame it on the heavy clay that fills my garden. Despite the fact that I added several tonnes of topsoil to it just a few years ago (and my garden is tiny), it remains the stuff from which pots, rather than potatoes, are made. My only spade is currently bent out of shape because I tried to dig a small hole to plant a fern. That's the hallmark of my garden: it is resistant to change. It will destroy your tools and your patience, and whatever you plant will most likely die anyway. It's nearly impossible to put down roots.

If it hasn't rained for a while, then you might as well forget about the spade, bent or not. The ground sets hard in dry spells, making it completely impenetrable. After a while, it cracks. It takes a lot of rain to get it right again. I have learned that the best possible strategy is negligence. The plants that grow there have to do it by choice; my intervention is unwanted. Anything I do plant needs to have solid roots. When all that topsoil went in, I planted a load of native hedging whips – birch, rowan and cobnut – and left them to make their own miniature woodland. I threw in some bluebell bulbs, which are only just beginning to appear (and then sparsely), and I decided to let the garden make up its own mind when it came to the rest. I stopped fighting. I let it run wild.

Well, almost wild. Whitstable is locked in a perpetual battle with couch grass, and so I sometimes have to pull up a great carpet of the stuff, because it would choke out anything else. Bindweed, too, is a problem. In high summer, it creeps across the patio at what seems to be a rate of a yard a day, and it took down two of my little tree saplings by winding around the narrow trunks and then cracking them in half. I now gather up big handfuls of it

whenever I go outside. But that's the limit of my weed-
ing. The left-hand side of the plot is taken over by bushes
of euphorbia, with its lime-green flowers and firework
leaves. It's an attractive plant, but probably not in the
quantity I have it. However, I spent a few years trying to
grub it up, and it always returns. I'm leaving it be, and
I'm now choosing the same strategy with the periwinkle
that creeps under my fence on the opposite side. I don't
really like it, and the dog often growls at it for no reason,
but I've noticed that the more I fight it, the more vigor-
ously it grows. I have conceded defeat.

What I like very much is the clump of dark purple hellebores that overhang the patio. I planted them alongside
clouds of forget-me-nots, which of course all died, but the
hellebores remain. Every year I cut a few for a vase and
regret it: they wither in moments. They're best left in the
soil alongside the silvery lamb's ears, which I think are a
relic from a previous owner, and the enormous feverfews,
which arrive in increasing numbers every year. I suppose
they're technically a weed, but I like their frilled leaves
and bobbing white flowers. There's some mint in there,
if you hunt for it, and some sad-looking rosemary, too. I
can persuade neither to bolt. There's also a fair amount
of sticky weed, which I like – it's sculptural and fun to
throw at Bert – and every few summers, borage runs ram-
pant for reasons I don't understand. That's the sum total

of it. It's not a neat garden, but the bees like it, and most of the time I think I do, too.

The wildflower seeds never came up, or not as far as I can tell among the rest of the jumble anyway. I'm honestly not sure I'd notice either way. But in an alleyway a hundred yards from my house, someone else has clearly planted their packet of seeds properly. Each April, the wildflowers arrive in a narrow patch of ground alongside the path, and by summer they make a riotous display. There are poppies, cornflowers and calendula. There is wild scabious and viper's bugloss. There is Queen Anne's lace, the white umbellifer with a single red flower in the middle, said to be a drop of Queen Anne's blood when she pricked her finger as she sewed. As soon as the ground warms, they all push themselves up through the dirt and remind us of the sheer exuberance of life, the way that it somehow always finds a way to thrive, even when it is constrained and in a dark corner. Even if that exuberance has to happen sideways, through cracks in the concrete.

I had to look up some of those plant names the first time they grew. The knowledge was not native to me. The poppies and cornflowers gave me no trouble, and the scabious I knew because my grandmother used to point them out as a flower she had in her wedding bouquet. When the time came, I had them in my posy, too, because we all find ways to mark a lineage in what we do. The wiry spikes of viper's bugloss spring up at the far end of the beach each summer, and the name delighted me the first time I heard it. It used to be used to treat adder bites, and so it bears a range of snaky names: adderwort, viper's herb and viper's grass. It is the most unreal, over-saturated blue, not quite purple.

Naming wildflowers is a long-standing mission of mine. I own a pile of second-hand field guides and have a phone app, which is usually less effective, and I do my best to discover the name of any new plant I notice. The noticing part is infinite: you start with the more obvious – the more showy flowers and the trees – and then, grad-ually, you notice the quieter species, too. Some are tiny, and some are just part of the general carpet of green that rises up in the spring. The natural world never stops giv-ing you detail to observe.

But this learning seems to be a perpetual cycle of for-getting. Every year I lose half of what I took in, as if my brain, in an act of energy preservation, flushes out superfluous facts during winter. The following year, I will return to dimly remembered plants and say, 'This one smells like cologne,' or 'This one's leaves taste of onion,' but I will have no memory of the name. Meanwhile, some names have been divorced from any recollection of their appearance. They swarm around my mind like flies while I walk in the woods, and I wonder how I could have known this only three seasons ago. I am frustrated the most by the umbellifers, one of which (giant hogweed) can burn the skin, and one of which (hemlock) is poisonous. It seems to me that it would be useful to recall the difference between these and cow parsley as I'm brushing my hand over their floating heads when I'm out on summer walks. But apparently, my brain considers this to be disposable information. I must google them every spring.

Naming is a form of power. It cements a commitment to the subject of your expertise and, in the case of nature, often an ancestral continuity, too. Naming is an assertion of meaning, and in turn it creates meaning. It allows us to greet the things we know like old friends. In Ursula K. Le Guin's Earthsea books, naming and magic are intertwined, with new wizards studying the true name of every living thing in Old Speech, the language of dragons. When you can name something, you have power over it, and acts of alchemy are possible if you change the true name of an object. In this reality, names are an elemental force of their own, a by-product of creation. As the protagonist, Ged, says: 'My name, and yours, and the true name of the sun, or a spring of water, or an unborn child, all are syllables of the great word that is very slowly spoken by the shining of the stars.'

One great word, spoken by the shining of the stars. It reminds me a lot of *OM*, the single syllable from which

the universe is created. Both are just ways of conceptu-
alising a foundational fact of living. The alchemy comes
in understanding the truth that is so easily hidden: that
everything is interconnected. That there is only one
whole. That we exist within a system that includes every
degraded human act and every beautiful one, every blade
of grass and every mountain; that shines and snaps and
varies like the surface of the sea. We as individuals contain it all. We hold within us the potential for the greatest
good and the most dreadful evil. We know, intuitively,
how each feels, because there are lines traced between us
and everything else. I don't have to believe in God as a
person. I can believe in this instead: the entire mesh of
existence binding us together in ways we perceive only
if we listen. Each of us is a particle of this greater entity.
Each one of us contains it all.

We find this absolute connectedness hard to grasp. We
often prefer to forget it. We often push back against it.
But it is there, real as sunlight, behind everything we do.
Since it is too big for us to swallow whole, we approach
it through metaphor. We tell stories about monsters and
magic and elemental gods, but really we are finding a way
to understand. Really we are talking about us, all of us
together. Some of the old stories don't work anymore. We
are finding them harder and harder to understand. But
that doesn't mean we abandon them. Instead, we need to

double down on the storytelling, and find new ways to tell out our meanings. Perhaps that is what we're meant to do: remake our stories until we finally find the one that fits.

God has always been a name whispered between us.

☾

I am told that in Singapore, the dandelions so often cursed by English gardeners are traded on eBay for good money. Those who buy them are in awe of the delicate orbs of their seed heads and admire the bounty of a plant whose leaves and petals are both edible. What is invisible in one place is beautiful in another. We even degrade them in their naming – in colloquial English, a dandelion (itself deriving from *dent de lion*, or lion's tooth, referring to its jagged leaves) is a wet-the-bed.

I think I've always loved dandelions as much as the Singaporeans, possibly because I've never much revered a pristine lawn. They are choked out in my back garden, but they spring up from the cracks in the path that lead to my front door, and I haven't yet lost the thrill of blowing dandelion clocks to tell the time, one huff of breath for each hour. One o'clock, two o'clock . . . When all the seeds are gone, you check your watch, and the time should match. It never fails, but then the thing about a dandelion is that a few wisps of floss always cling to the stem, which means you can finesse your time-telling. When you reach the correct time, you can claim that those last few seeds won't ever come away. For the higher numbers, you can just keep on blowing.

Flowers are, after all, made from air. Remove their source of water, which needs to be constantly replenished, and most of what is left is carbon. The skeleton of the flower is built from this molecule, absorbed from the carbon dioxide that we exhale. It is surprising what can be made from something that seems so thin.

We, who so often think we're cultureless, can unpack a galaxy of stories from one garden weed. But the time has come for us to understand what these stories mean to us, and to reconnect with the other stories, too, which are all waiting for us in our gardens and surging up from the cracks in the pavement. We must tell them to our children, so that they can't imagine living without them. Telling them is an act of belonging, a way of pushing taproots deep into the ground. In a world full of restless and displaced people, it's an act of welcome, too. When we tell the stories of the things that inhabit our land, we help newcomers to read the deep terrain around them and perhaps to feel a little more at home. And storytelling is always an exchange: when we listen to what is told to us, we enrich our mythology. We get closer to the big, beautiful, metaphorical whole.

EPILOGUE: AETHER

Each year the Lyrid meteor shower appears at the end of April, as the earth passes into the orbit of comet C/1861 G1 (Thatcher), burning up the debris it leaves behind. Their radiant is next to the constellation of Lyra, the lyre of Orpheus, placed in the sky by an eagle on Zeus's command. Because Thatcher has a relatively short orbital period, returning every four hundred and fifteen years, the meteors are particularly bright and fast, and have the reputation among starwatchers of putting on a good display.

I have never once seen them. Have you? There are twelve regular meteor showers reliably happening above our heads each year, and yet few of us ever make the effort to watch. I know, I know: it's hard. They happen late at night, and when it's dark and cold, and we live surrounded by light pollution and can barely see the sky at all. And there are clouds and rainstorms, and there's work in the morning. But still: meteors. Shooting stars. Those streaks of light we find so magical that we invest them with our wishes. Surely that's a sight worthy of effort?

In medieval philosophy, the earth was made of four elements – earth, water, fire and air – but the vast universe beyond it was composed of a different substance entirely. This was aether, a particularly refined material that transcended the states we recognise. Known as the quintessence, it was neither hot nor cold, neither wet nor dry, and was capable of changing its density. It was the stuff from which stars were made, and light, and gravity. It tended naturally towards circular motion and so set the orbits of the planets.

Did the sky lose a little of its magic when we came to understand that celestial bodies are made of exactly the same molecules that we find on earth? Perhaps. But then the night sky has now become rare in a different way, fading from view beyond the electric glow of modern life. On a clear night, so long as the people in the house that backs onto ours have not turned on their security light, the stars are bright and multitudinous. If the security light is on, all bets are off. You can barely see the rest of the garden, let alone the firmament. But even without this, it's hard to escape the seep of street lamps and the bright displays of local shops that cause enough light pollution to obscure the night sky, leaving only the largest stars visible. Our love of electric light is leaching some of the wonder from the world. If I want to see a meteor storm – and I do – then I'll need to travel.

The UK has a handful of Dark Sky Reserves, where lighting is controlled to protect dark spaces. This includes the islands of Coll and Sark, where whole communities have agreed to forgo outside lighting in favour of basking in the full glow of the Milky Way. But travelling in constrained times, I had to suppress my desire to go to the farthest reaches of the British Isles in search of perfect darkness. Instead, I chose the three-hundred-mile drive to Exmoor, which I knew would also soothe my heartfelt longing for my favourite coastline.

Embarking on a ten-hour round trip to see some meteors really brings home our attitude towards enchanting things. When I tell people what I'm doing, they say, 'Wow, can you do that?' and then, also, 'Why are you bothering?' The time between those two responses is usually infinitesimally small. We are awed in principle by what is out there, but we prefer to keep that awe theoretical unless it drops into our laps. Meteors sit perfectly on the cusp of the mundane and the rare. They are there, but only if we seek them out. We know that if we encounter them, it will be a remarkable experience, perhaps even one we will remember for years to come. But because of that very ordinariness, we defer going out to look for them. After all, no one else is doing it. It's not an event, like a solar eclipse. We would feel silly for making a fuss about it. It would be a childish thing, and we are adults.

We don't concern ourselves with shooting stars.

I think I'm beginning to understand that the quest is the point. Our sense of enchantment is not triggered only by grand things; the sublime is not hiding in distant landscapes. The awe-inspiring, the numinous, is all around us, all the time. It is transformed by our deliberate attention. It becomes valuable when we value it. It becomes meaningful when we invest it with meaning. The magic is of our own conjuring. Hierophany – that revelation of the sacred – is something that we bring to everyday things, rather than something that is given to us. That quality of experience that reveals to us the workings of the world, that comforts and innervates us, that ushers us towards a greater understanding of the business of being human: it is not in itself rare. What is rare is our will to pursue it. If we wait passively to become enchanted, we could wait a long time.

But seeking is a kind of work. I don't mean heading off on wild road trips just to see the stars that are shining above your own roof. I mean committing to a lifetime of engagement: to noticing the world around you, to actively looking for small distillations of beauty, to making time to contemplate and reflect. To learning the names of the plants and places that surround you, or training your mind in the rich pathways of the metaphorical. To finding a way to express your interconnectedness with the rest of

humanity. To putting your feet on the ground, every now
and then, and feeling the tingle of life that the earth offers
in return. It's all there, waiting for our attention. Take off
your shoes, because you are always on holy ground.

It is already two days past the peak of the Lyrids when we
head out into the night to find them. Bert takes an early
bath, and we put him in the car dressed in pyjamas and
a hoodie, ready to crawl straight into bed when we get
back. He's now past the age when I could carry his sleeping form out of the car, and I miss it even as we're making
plans. With the sun low in the sky, we drive out of the town
where we've rented a house and into the wilds of Exmoor,
roads narrowing and acres of wild scrubland stretching
out before us. The greener fields are full of ewes and their
lambs, and in some places they fill the roadside verges,
too, chewing on the grass and shedding their wool all over
the prickly gorse. A few of the sturdier lambs try their luck
against the car, holding their ground in the middle of the
road as we crawl towards them and then bounding off in
a clatter of ungainly legs at the last moment.

The drive takes us so high that our ears pop, and we
share a packet of Polo mints to regain our equilibrium.
When I booked this trip, I didn't count on a supermoon.
Rising already in the sky, the moon is within 90 per cent

of her perigee, the astronomical term for the point in her orbit that's closest to the earth. This means that she will be unusually bright tonight. I am hoping that this will not be fatal to my meteor viewing prospects, drowning out the paler light of the stars. She is gibbous, though – a 'humpback' moon, not quite yet full. In just a couple of days, she will be the milk moon, opening the Anglo-Saxon month of *þrimilcemōnaþ*, the month of three milkings. This is the beginning of summer, when the eighth-century monk Bede noted that our ancestors milked their cows three times a day, a season of fecundity and relief from the wastes of winter. That sense of liberation is still tangible for us now. Freed from the dark months that have kept us indoors, we can now strive out into the night in search of wonder. We feel it all the more keenly after a year of staying home.

We park at Holdstone Down and walk uphill along a stony path as the sky darkens. Above my head, the aether is a thin blue, streaking orange towards the horizon. As we reach the crest, the land falls away before us, giving way to a restless grey sea and a ladder of cliffs fading into the distance. Bert is fascinated by the cairn that sits at the peak of the hill, the first one he's seen. He's got lucky. Most of the cairns I've ever come across have been at the summit of a long climb or in a spot so remote that walkers have felt compelled to mark the occasion of their passing

through. We had to walk for only five minutes. The pile
of stones is as tall I am, and probably fifteen feet in diam-
eter. At the very top, someone has arranged a miniature
stack of three stones, forming an arch through which I
can glimpse a segment of the sky.

Cairns are spontaneous, shifting monuments to a hundred different things. A bunch of browning flowers is
secured under one of the stones, facing seaward. I show
Bert that he can add a stone of his own, and he does, and
then adds one for every member of his family: for me, for
Daddy, for Grandma, for the cats and for the dog – all the
beings he treasures. And just like that, he makes his own
ritual, an act of invention and a gesture of connection. He
doesn't need to be shown this. He knows already. What
he needs, as he grows older, is continuing permission to
map meaning across the landscape.

Later, when I look up cairns on the internet, I find a
glut of annoyed comments that they pile over ancient
monuments or contravene the ethic of 'leave no trace' –
that they are yet another way in which humans impose
their unwanted presence on the wild. I think that speaks
more about our disenchantment than it does about our
destructiveness. Stones added to ancient sites of ritual
suggest to me that there's a continuity of practice at play,
a river of meaning that has flowed through the centuries.
Leaving a trace is not necessarily the same as doing harm,

especially when it merely involves the shifting of stones from one place to another. Making these connections will surely usher us into more careful stewardship of the land on which we walk.

It is time to reject these false breaks between ancient irrational humanity, whose beliefs we would commit to distant history, and the modern subject, bereft of meaning; between the idea of pure nature and the unruly people who pass through it. We don't destroy colonial attitudes about the landscape by erasing people from it altogether, and forbidding their ever-morphing acts of meaning-making. We don't preserve our natural landscapes by turning them into a museum. We heal these rifts by inviting back gentleness into our relationship with the earth, by allowing meaning to take hold again. We should encourage enchantment to bolt like a weed. It is, after all, native here. The stones, and the dried-out heather, and the sound of the sea, and the moon above our heads have all been storing it like a battery, waiting for its current to be found again.

The wind has picked up and the sky still isn't dark, so we pad back down the path to the car. There are no stars yet, and the moon is now high and invasively bright. H remembers a lay-by a little further along the road where he thinks we'll have a better view of Lyra. According to an app on my phone, the constellation is now rising to the north-east, still low in the sky. We drive a little way and park again. Turning off all the lights, we watch the sky darken through the windows, and we see the first stars come out.

Bert has never had the chance to watch the first specks of light appear and then to notice the paler stars gradually become visible all around them. I can never tell whether this happens because the sky is getting incrementally blacker or whether you just get your eye in. Probably a little of both. Either way, he's so excited by it that he's chattering and fidgeting in the back seat, rattling my seat. It's way past his bedtime already, and I can see that he won't last a lot longer. I'm craving silence, the chance to feel my way into this moment, but it's not possible. We get out, wrap up warm, and perch on the car's bonnet to look across the sea. It is still not dark enough for Lyra to be visible. There's a pale band just above the horizon, and across the water, the lights of Swansea are twinkling. A little way along the coast, I can see the regular pulse of the lighthouse at Foreland Point. There is too much light. There is not enough darkness. Meanwhile, the moon is a menace, shining so fervently that a veil is cast across the whole sky. It is cold, and the wind is in my ears, and I've come all this way for absolutely nothing, for an invisible starfall.

And then I notice it, pooling at our feet. I say to H,

'You've left the headlights on. No wonder we can't see anything.' But as he shifts to find his keys, I realise that the lights are not on. So where do they come from, the shadows that flow down the cliff from our shoes? It takes me a few beats to realise that it must be the moon.

'Look!' I say to Bert. 'Our moon shadow!'

We are, collectively, a little bit amazed, and we step left and right, and raise our arms to prove it's really true. H and I both break into song, though I choose Cat Stevens and he opts for Mike Oldfield, and there is momentary confusion as our voices clash. But then we watch quietly. Night is already a shadow cast on the side of the earth that has turned away from the sun. This is a shadow within a shadow, a fragile thing made by moonlight. I can't remember ever seeing mine before. Perhaps I have and I haven't noticed. Perhaps I've never found the right darkness before. Perhaps I wasn't ready for it to unpack its meaning as it does for me here and now. I have gone looking for one thing and found another, not something rare and celestial and beyond my control, but something that was always within my power to find. The act of seeking attuned my senses and primed my mind to make associations. I was open to magic, and I found some, although not the magic I was looking for. That's what you find over and over again when you go looking: something else. An insight that surprises you.

A connection that you would never have made. A new perspective.

More often than not, I find that I already hold all the ideas from which my enchantment is made. The deliberate pursuit of attention, ritual, or reflection does not mystically draw in anything external to me. Instead, it creates experiences that rearrange what I know to find the insights I need today. This is how symbolic thought works. It offers you a repository of understanding that can be triggered by the everyday, and which comes in a format that goes straight to the bloodstream. I don't have words to describe what it meant to play with my moon shadow. Instead, I feel it in my body, a kind of physical wonder at what is there waiting for me when I stop to notice.

Do I detect a divine sense of humour behind this world that allows me to drive for five hours to be enthralled by something I could find in my own backyard? Or it is my own amusement reflected back at me, as I am taught something I already know, but which apparently bears repeating? I don't think it matters. In fact I think I prefer a strange tangle of both, an idea with porous boundaries that keeps me guessing. We are not offered any definite conclusions, only the continuing quest. Certainties harden us, and eventually we come to defend them as if the world can't contain a multiplicity of views. We are better off staying soft. It gives us room to grow and absorb, to make space for all the other glorious notions that will keep coming at us across a lifetime.

Bert gets back into the car, and I know I don't have long here now. If he falls asleep in the back seat, I'll have to wake him when we get home, and I know how miserable that feels. I squint out at the horizon and the stars seem to double with my efforts. I can see the slant square of Lyra clearly now, and below it the last dregs of daylight still lightening the far edge of the sea, this long after sunset. There is a boat bobbing out there, its light moving rhythmically with the swell. In my peripheral vision, I think I see a streak of white light, barely discernible, fleeting. My eyes flick back to the part of the sky where it appeared, but there is nothing there.

Did I see a shooting star, or was it the desperate imaginings of tired eyes? It doesn't matter either way. I get to choose what I make of it. This is exactly where I want to be: watching the skies for a glimpse of starfall.

ACKNOWLEDGEMENTS

I wasn't exaggerating when I said I ran out of charge. Writing *Enchantment* sometimes felt like dragging a deadweight (me) up a very steep hill (language itself), and I'm so grateful to everyone who helped to lighten the load, through many false starts and wrong turns. These pages are dedicated to them:

To Laura Hassan for taking me on, and bringing so much passion, wisdom and steadiness.

To the incredible team at Faber & Faber: Hannah Knowles, Hannah Marshall and Hannah Turner, Mo Hafeez, Sara Cheraghlou, Donna Payne, Anne Owen, Barbara Mignocchi, Sara Talbot, Sarah Davison-Aitkins, Mallory Ladd and the dedicated Faber sales reps.

To Jynne Dilling Martin, who patiently shaped this book as I stumbled through many, many drafts.

To Jennie Speedy for swimming with me, Kate Fox for walking with me, Clare Jackson for taking me on pilgrimages. To the Zen Peacemakers for taking me on a journey, and to Rami Efal for helping me get there.

To Angela Y. Walton-Raji, Paul Koubek and Quinn Brett for giving their time to talk to me while I was doing my initial research, and to Richard Ashcroft for patiently explaining why my original idea couldn't possibly work.

To Maddy Milburn for being an astute agent and a treasured friend, and to her brilliant team, especially Rachel Yeoh and Liv Maidment, Hannah Ladds and Giles Milburn. To Liane-Louise Smith, Georgina Simmonds and Valentina Paulmichl for sending my words all over the world.

To H and Bert, who willingly get dragged along on wild adventures, and sometimes even enjoy them.

To my readers and Patreons, who make this real.

PERMISSIONS CREDITS

Page 46: lines from 'Go to the Limits of Your Longing' from *Rilke's Book of Hours: Love Poems to God* by Rainer Maria Rilke, translated by Anita Barrows and Joanna Macy, translation copyright © 1996 by Anita Barrows and Joanna Macy. Used by permission of Riverhead, an imprint of Penguin Publishing Group, a division of Penguin Random House LLC. All rights reserved.

Page 111: from *Chants of a Lifetime* (2010), p. 187, lines from chant 'The Gates of Sweet Nectar' from Krishna Das's song, 'Calling Out to Hungry Hearts', published by Hay House, Inc., Carlsbad, CA.

Page 125: lines from 'Encounter' in *New and Collected Poems* (2001) by Czeslaw Milosz, courtesy of HarperCollins Publishers.

Quotations on pp. 160 and 206 are from *Parable of the Sower* in Olivia E. Butler's Earthseed series and from *A Wizard of Earthsea* in Ursula K. Le Guin's Earthsea series, respectively.